A Vacationer's Guide to Rural New England Bookstores

A Vacationer's Guide to Rural New England Bookstores

Connecticut
Maine
Massachusetts
Cape Cod
New Hampshire
Rhode Island
Vermont – Northern
Vermont - Southern

by
Richard F. Wright

New England Bookstore Publishing
Jefferson, Massachusetts
Web: GuideToNewEnglandBookstores.com
Blog: Richard-Wright.blogspot.com

Published by
Bookstand Publishing
Morgan Hill, CA 95037
3762_3

ISBN 978-1-61863-388-0

Printed in the United States of America

PREFACE

This is the Guide Book I wished I had during the past 40 years while vacationing in New England. Wherever I ventured, to the shore, the mountains, the lakes, or the attractions, eventually I looked for the nearest bookstore for entertainment, information, and inspiration.

I hope you will find this guide useful as you venture into the New England region and especially if you find yourself in the rural parts of the various states in search of a full-service, independent, or antiquarian book shop.

It's always been my opinion that part of the pleasure of being on vacation is the change of routine. While on vacation you may wake up at a different time, you may eat different food, you may even make purchase decisions unlike those at home. At home, if I decide to look for a book about Revolutionary War uniforms, I can use the Internet to find sources of background information, identify dealers of specialty books, and make a direct purchase online. For many a bibliophile, that's good enough.

But, when I'm on vacation, I actually don't want to log onto the computer at all – if I can avoid it. I much prefer to pop into a local, rural bookstore and browse the aisles of publisher overstocks and glance through the "local writers" shelf for books about the area I am vacationing in that summer. But, to pop in, I need to know where the shop is. If the guide in your hand succeeds, it will help you plan your spontaneous visits to rural New England bookstores.

ACKNOWLEDGEMENTS

Each of the bookstores that I mention has been a resource for me over the years, without any of them realizing that I was writing a guide book for vacationers. Over the years, a few of them have found my blog or heard about the previous edition of the book, but it was not widely distributed and somewhat unknown. I thank each of them, not for helping with the guide, but for being the dedicated, thoughtful, sincere book shop operators I have visited over the years.

My wife Patti has endured my passion for books, bookstores and reading, only because she likes to read too. She may not spend the hours in a bookstore that I do, but she lets me do it without complaint and I'm grateful for that. (I try to pick up a book or two for her as I go along; seems like the sensible thing to do).

Parnassus Book Service – Yarmouthport MA – (Cape Cod)

INTRODUCTION

Can the Rural New England Booksellers Defeat the National Trend in Bookstore Closings?

Sadly, I continue to come across articles on the Internet from various newspapers around the country about another independent bookstore closing. Once in a while a chain-store shop closes, but more often than not, it's an independent. The story always has similar threads. The owner of many years has seen a steady decline in sales without hope of reversing the trend. Frequently, there is no one else in the family interested in continuing the business. Attempts to sell have failed and the final decision is to close. In 2011 the *Ben Franklin Bookstore* in Worcester closed as the owner felt he couldn't run a brick and mortar store anymore. He continues to offer his collection via the Internet. During my recent visits around New England I found stores closed that I thought were still open.

Some of the authors of these articles have commented on the influence of Internet-based shopping, such as Amazon.com, the influx of chain-based bookstores, such as Barnes & Noble and the perceived overall decline in reading as contributors to the onslaught of independent bookstore closings. It probably shouldn't come as a surprise that this trend away from independent store owners has hit the bookseller just as much as neighborhood groceries, local sandwich shops, local pharmacies and other owner-operated enterprises. It's very difficult in the modern age to compete with the efficiencies of the chain or box store. Look what Home Depot and Lowe's did to the local lumber yard.

But, in New England, I have detected an extra heartiness among the independent booksellers. The rural New England bookstore has managed to succeed into the new age without compromising too much of its rural charm. The successful and appealing local booksellers are the ones that merge the online sale of books with the brick and mortar attractions.

Where necessary, the local, rural New England bookstore offers the CD's, the café, the Wi-Fi and other modern accoutrements that allow them to compete with the chain and box versions of the old-fashioned, rural, neighborhood bookstore; all this without sacrificing the sometimes esoteric, charming, personal touch many of us enjoy at the local, rural New England bookshop.

Without any scientific or statistical basis for making any claims, I would offer one observer's opinion that the *Toadstool Bookstores* in Peterborough, NH and Milford, NH are not likely to become threatened by a box store. They maintain enough rural distance to not be attractive to the chain store, which thrives in the denser population areas. Now, the Toadstool bookstore in Keene, NH faces the challenge of a box store already in place. But, the community is certainly large enough and vibrant enough to support these two stores, plus a few others that co-exist in Keene. Even so, the Toadstool shop in Keene moved its location downstairs within the mill store to smaller quarters. This reduced their overhead, presented itself to the customer better, and shows they are willing to adjust to meet competition.

So, what are the prospects for closings? I see them as unlikely in the near future. The strength of these independents rests in their location, their commitment to stocking what the community is looking for, their creativity in inventory and presentation, all of which, keep the customers coming back. While we have them, the local, rural New England bookstore is a treat. It's a place to satisfy the need to hold a book in your hand, surprise yourself with a used book at a tremendous bargain, (which you had been meaning to read for years) and a place where you can maintain a bit of community contact, not otherwise likely to happen at Mr. Big Box.

In its January 9, 2008 edition, in its Travel section, *USA Today* selected nine bookstores across the country that it considered worthy as a tourist "destination." Not just a place to visit while doing something else – but, as a reason to get on a plane, train or automobile and seek out the designated bookseller. They asked the question, "When is a bookstore worth a tourist's time"? Their answer was "When it's more than just a place where you can buy books."

By that definition, to be a "destination" for a tourist or anyone interested in more than just grabbing the latest best-seller, the "destination" bookstore must offer something not available at a cookie-cutter chain-store or just a click-away on the Internet (free shipping included). It must offer the tactile, aromatic, convivial something only available at your neighborhood, rural, locally-owned independent bookstore. For each of us, it's something different and probably not well defined. But, as the famous Supreme Court Justice Potter Stewart said about pornography, "I know it when I see it."

For me, that's what keeps the successful independent bookstore operating during these highly competitive times for small retailers. It's the reason why I believe that the New England bookstore will defeat the trend in closings suffered recently by independent booksellers.

As recently as June 2011 a new independent bookstore opened in W. Boylston MA, called *Beech Tree Place Bookstore*. The owner, Ina, had closed a record store a few years earlier and now expanded into a record and book shop. After a year of getting a foothold, the shop is doing well. To keep her growth plan in place she is moving this fall to Clinton, closer to home and expanded space at lower cost. Now, that's a trend I like to support.

This is part of the new alignment of small town book shops bringing the local customer and the tourist something the big box store can't. Back in 2005, *Where the Sidewalk Ends* opened in Chatham MA on Cape Cod. It did so while also flying in the face of the closing trend. Today, it is as vibrant a part of Main Street as any other shop in town.

By the way, the *USA Today* article did not include any booksellers in New England as a top "destination" book shop. Well, for my sake, that's not a bad thing. Why? Well, because it leaves my book, *A Vacationer's Guide to Rural New England Bookstores*, your single best source to find an excellent "destination bookstore," in New England. I wrote the first edition of this book in 2008 as a treat for myself demonstrating that there were plenty of bookstores in New England to meet my needs and the needs of many book readers and book collectors. This edition lists my favorite 39 full-service bookstores and my 25 favorite used book shops, plus a lot of honorable mentions.

My readers should remember that I haven't visited all the bookstores in New England. To my own amazement, I find shops wherever I go that I am unfamiliar with and become "new" to me. Discovery is a fun part of bookstore hunting. Also, I cheated a bit by separating Cape Cod from Massachusetts, in effect creating a seventh New England state (although others may agree with that concept for other reasons) because there are so many great bookstores on the Cape. I also split Vermont into Southern and Northern, because there were so many.

Finally, for the vacationer, or the native New Englander taking a day trip, I have included some of my favorite One-Day-Bookstore-Tours. Each one has three or four or more shops to visit in a single day, either as a destination or as an alternative to a rainy summer day, or snowless winter day (skiers have off-days too).

My website keeps the list fresh between book editions, so check for updates at GuideToNewEnglandBookstores.com. Or, visit my blog to see which stores I have visited lately at Richard-Wright.blogspot.com.

Traveler Book Cellar – Union CT

Contents

INDEPENDENT BOOKSTORES

USED-RARE BOOK SHOPS

ONE-DAY BOOKSTORE-TOURS

INDEPENDENT BOOKSTORES

My Favorite Full-Service Bookstores

The 39 bookstores listed in this section of the Guide are full-service, independent bookstores that I view as my favorites. On my website I commented that I could have selected 50 favorites or maybe one hundred. But, for the vacationer in New England, these choices will let you find a good book and a bit of the charm that independent, rural, New England bookstores have to offer in a shop near typical vacation destinations.

While on vacation you may not need the bookstore to order a book for you, but you might be looking for the newest release or an expanded collection of children's books for the kids. A children's book could be handy for a rainy day or the long ride home after vacation is over. And, a good, local bookstore may have that perfect gift to bring home or the local author book that reminds you of the wonderful time the family had.

The Vermont Book Shop – Middlebury VT

Chapter One

Bookstores in Connecticut

My favorite full-service bookstores in Connecticut are:
- *Bank Square Books – Mystic*
- *Breakwater Books – Guilford*
- *Elm Street Books – New Canaan*
- *R.J. Julia Booksellers – Madison*

If it appears I favor the coastline, I have to admit that's true. I have lived in Connecticut in the past, along the coast, and although I worked in Norwich, New London, and Hartford during those years, it was the shoreline that always attracted me.

During the years I worked and lived in Connecticut, I mostly lived in a sea Captain's house in Mystic. I would drive to work in Rhode Island at first, but mercifully, I found jobs nearer to my apartment that cut down on the commute. But, that left more time for exploring and the coast was where I spent my time. Ranging all the way to the Stamford area I became familiar with a lot of great book shops. Some are gone now, but among my favorites are the ones listed here.

Bank Square Books
The sea Captain's house that I rented in Mystic was only a few steps from Main Street, which is where *Bank Square Books* operates today. The feisty and fiercely independent store owners have endured, along with the rest of the town, the interminable refurbishing of the downtown hardscape. In the end I hope it

proves beneficial, but I understand the anguish everyone has endured during the long-delayed municipal improvement project.

Once you clamber over the loose brick work in front of the store, the experience is all positive. The book shelves are organized and labeled well, with a great children's section carefully selected for all ages. My nieces have appreciated that over the years.

Bank Square Books – Mystic

Bank Square Books is aggressive in sponsoring Author visits, which is not something easily done. Unless you are a regular visitor to book signings, you may not realize how hard it is to coordinate, promote and sustain interest. The mark of a truly dedicated local, independent bookstore is the on-going commitment to bringing the writer into contact with the reader.

Breakwater Books

In Guilford, again along the coast, resides *Breakwater Books*. This book shop has been around for four decades on the Green in Guilford. The blue awning is distinctive among the shops along the street. The bookstore features a

Breakwater Books – Guilford

large children's section and offers a strong selection of local authors. They feature book signings, which are important for creating a sense of participation for customers. If it's going to be the local source for books, it's great to see your neighbors at the shop to meet authors.

Elm Street Books

About six years ago, *Elm Street Books* reopened with the help of some of its more influential neighbors, including a major television personality, and the result has been a successful rebirth of a great local book shop. The residents of the town try to keep the New England feel while obviously relying on the economic strength of nearby

Elm Street Books – New Canaan

New York City and its many opportunities. This shop brings all of the current best sellers, but also works hard to bring some of the local flair to the selections.

R.J. Julia Independent Booksellers

Another favorite general bookstore in Connecticut is *R.J. Julia Independent Booksellers* in Madison, CT. This place simply rocks. I can't imagine a book shop that holds as many varied events each year as they do. Local authors, internationally famous authors, readings, book clubs, and children's story times are all part of the atmosphere. The booksellers who work here

R.J. Julia Booksellers – Madison

are eager to write about and tell you personally what they have been reading and why they liked it. It's comforting to have some input when there is so much to read and almost never enough

3

time to read it all. A little advice from your friends at R.J. Julia goes a long way.

I am also a fan of how much space they devote to placing books face-out, so you can read the whole cover to save my sore neck from reading the spines with my head down between my knees. And after you buy your book, magazine or gift card, you have almost too many places on the street to pull up a chair, have a cool drink and a snack while you start reading your new book.

Bank Square Books
53 West Main Street
Mystic, CT 06355
Tel: 860-536-3795
Web: banksquarebooks.com

Breakwater Books
81 Whitfield Street
Guilford, CT 06437
Tel: 203-453-4141
Web: breakwaterbooks.net

Elm Street Books
35 Elm Street
New Canaan CT 06840
Tel: 203-966-4545
Web: elmstreetbooks.com

R.J. Julia Bookseller
768 Boston Post Road
Madison, CT 06443
Tel: 203-245-3959
Web: rjjulia.com

Chapter Two

Bookstores in Maine

My favorite full-service bookstores in Maine are:
- *Sherman's Books – Bar Harbor*
  (Boothbay, Camden, Freeport)
- *Hello, Hello Books – Rockland*
- *Maine Coast Book Shop – Damariscotta*
- *Blue Hill Books – Blue Hill*

Once again, the coastline draws me in. The vacation destinations for us in Maine are generally along the coast. Except for the occasional trip to my sister's cabin in Caratunk, about 30 miles from the Canadian border, our visits are generally at the beaches from Ogunquit to Old Orchard all the way to Camden and Rockland.

We love to play golf and the Samoset Resort is one of a number of destinations for us when on a golf vacation. The book shops along the way up to Rockport, ME are boundless. I especially enjoy the specialty used book shops, but when you need a full-service bookshop, it's a pleasure to shop along the coast of Maine.

Sherman's Books
The *Sherman's Books* quartet of shops is a regular stop for us. Whenever we hit one of the towns where they have a branch location, we are sure to find something in the discount bin. When we are in Bar Harbor for a week I am sure to stop in daily. How

can that be? It's because the downtown location means we walk past it every day. "I'll only be a minute."

On the sidewalk outside the shop in Bar Harbor is a human-size lobster that just begs for tourists to pose next to. Yes, we posed each other for the silly photo-opportunity. It's part of the routine for visitors and we felt we had to.

The other Sherman's locations each have its own personality and its own selection of bargain books. It's not like a visit to a big-box bookstore where the aisles and the shelves are all matchy-match. The bargains in Camden are different than Freeport. (That's what I tell my wife so we have to visit them all.)

Hello Hello Books

We love Rockland. The place feels bigger than it is. The newly named *Hello Hello Books* bookstore is a testament to determination in the face of changing circumstances. The previous owner had to sell and the current owner stepped up after years of managing the shop when it was known as Rock City Books. The name is eclectic and I'm sure I'll get an explanation

Hello Hello Books – Rockland

for it the next time I stop in, but what could be friendlier than Hello?

During one visit to the shop I found a copy of a Stephen Ambrose volume about World War II. I have many or most of his books, but this was one I had not collected yet. It seemed that the $10 was fair for a book in great condition.

6

The Maine Coast Book Shop

Half way between Bath and Rockland is *The Maine Coast Book Shop* in Damariscotta. If I tell you Damariscotta is near

Newcastle, does that help? I love rural book shops. This certainly qualifies when you think about rural meaning not near a big city. My fascination with the shop is its continuity with several owners going back to the mid 1960's. That's endurance. Also, as I've

Maine Coast Book Shop – Damariscotta

mentioned elsewhere, when you add a café, as they did here about 10 years ago, or a record shop, or align yourself with other local shops, such as galleries, I have found the local independent shops can survive a little longer.

The Maine Coast Book Shop staff offer suggestions of books they have read and like, plus they place an emphasis on local authors. The shop offers a range of book signings during the year.

Blue Hill Books

When you talk about rural in New England, this is what should come to mind. This little town has the *North Light Books, Red Gap Books,* and *Blue Hill Books.* With so many small towns without any bookstores, it's remarkable to find

Blue Hill Books – Blue Hill

three in such a small, rural location. At *Blue Hill Books*, the dirt

7

driveway and the front porch put you in the right mindset when you first enter. The hand-crafted bookshelves, built by the owner, are testament to the serious care given to book selection, display and selling. As a full-service bookseller, it's the place to stop to get the light summer reading or something for the kids. But, remember, the town has two used book shops to check out too.

Sherman's Books
56 Main Street
Bar Harbor ME
Tel: 207-288-3161
Web: Shermans.com
    Boothbay – 5 Commercial Street
    Camden – 14 Main Street
    Freeport – 148 Main Street

Hello Hello Books
316 Main Street
Rockland ME 04841
Tel: 207-593-7780
Web: hellohellobooks.com

Maine Coast Book Shop
158 Main Street
Damariscotta, ME 04543
Tel: 860-338-6850
Web: mainecoastbookshop.com

Blue Hill Books
26 Pleasant Street
Blue Hill ME 04614
Tel: 207-374-5632
Web: bluehillbooks.com

Chapter Three

Bookstores in Massachusetts (Part I)
(Not including Cape Cod)

My favorite full-service bookstores in Massachusetts are:
- *Andover Bookstore – Andover MA*
- *Concord Bookshop – Concord MA*
- *Jabberwocky Bookshop – Newburyport MA*
- *Tatnuck Bookseller – Westborough MA*
- *Odyssey Bookshop – South Hadley MA*

Andover Bookstore

When you walk into a store and there is a blazing fire in the stone fireplace, you know it's a different kind of place than you're likely to find at a mall. The *Andover Bookstore*, which was established in 1809, has a lot going for it to distinguish it from the modern retail outlet. Its multi-floor, slightly crowded, quirky layout is all part of being over 200 years old.

Andover Bookstore – Andover

For the bargain hunter in me, I found discounted books upstairs, which always salvages a bookshop for me. I'm not against paying full price or near-full price for the latest book, but, please help me out with a bargain so that I can stretch the book budget. The Andover Bookstore gets it. They have been increasing their efforts to bring used books into the shop.

9

Concord Bookshop

Over the years we have made many visits to the Lexington-Concord part of the state to visit the historic Revolutionary war memorials and sites. But, the fun continues in town for me when I get to visit the *Concord Bookshop*. It's a place where the employees really are book people. When I buy a book, someone will comment that they just read it and loved it or plan to read it next. When I hear that at the Concord Bookshop it rings true. They really are book people.

Concord Bookshop – Concord

The author signings area looks like the lounge area of an old fashioned gentlemen's club. No rickety card table shoved in the corner at this shop. The author and his listeners are treated as royalty here. The pre-promotion is strong and visible with a lot of successful book signings.

Jabberwocky Bookshop

On the North Shore, there are many great book shops. But, the one I like the most is the kitschy *Jabberwocky Bookshop* in Newburyport. Stuffed inside an old mill, along with a variety of other retail outlets, the shop is expansive and fun to shop in. The shelves are so tall that I can't read the books at the top. You have to climb a ladder to see everything. The bargain bins have color dots

Jabberwocky Bookshop – Newburyport

10

to code the discount. I like that. There is also a bargain room with remainders, which is always appealing. This shop qualifies as a destination bookseller because it offers the new books, the used books, the alliance with a children's toy shop, and a location that provides convenient parking, other quaint shops and an atmosphere that visitors are seeking during a day trip or a vacation stop-over.

Tatnuck Bookseller

After many years as a staple in the Worcester area, the *Tatnuck Bookseller* moved out of the city to the town of Westborough, which serves as a glorified bedroom community for Boston. I feared it would fade from its role as a strong independent, particularly when the founder sold the business to the landlord. But, happily after many years now it continues to be a favorite. The bestsellers are always discounted and discounting throughout the store is very strong. You will find books well organized and displayed and knowledgeable people ready to help. Plus you

Tatnuck Bookseller – Westborough

can buy a gift or a cup of coffee, which makes the shop a one-stop destination.

My family has taken to buying me gift cards to the Tatnuck Bookseller, instead of Home Depot, when they can't think of anything to buy me for my birthday and they are amazed when a $50 card nets me a dozen books or more. I have sharpened my shopping skills to maximize the amount of reading material I can acquire because of how well the shop merchandizes its books.

Odyssey Bookshop

As an Alumni of UMass/Amherst I try to visit "Happy Valley" as often as I can. This often brings me to one of my favorite booksellers, the *Odyssey Bookshop* in South Hadley. To be honest, I am more inclined to be bargain hunting up the road at the *Montague Bookmill* in Montague and the *Book Bear* in West Brookfield on the way home, but as long as I'm in the area, a visit to Odyssey Bookshop makes sense too.

The shop has been around a long time, and at its current location, for about 20 years. As part of a quaint mall setting, there is some built-in traffic that helps keep the shop lively. There are cafes, bistros, pubs, as well as a variety of retail outlets. Parents of

Odyssey Bookshop – South Hadley

students attending school nearby and tourists to the Pioneer Valley all find this a destination. The book shop helps drive traffic to the mall, but also benefits from the other shops nearby. It's a mutually beneficial arrangement.

In addition to its role as full-service book shop, it is the prime source for textbooks for students at Mount Holyoke College. In addition to an increasing commitment to used books, the store offers a signed First Edition club for those who like to collect books with the Author's signature.

Andover Bookstore
89 Main Street
Andover MA 01810
Tel: 978-475-0143
Web: hugobooks.com/andover

Concord Bookshop
65 Main Street
Concord MA
Tel: 978-369-2405
Web: concordbookshop.com

Jabberwocky Bookshop
50 Water Street
Newburyport MA 01950
Tel: 978-465-9359
Web: jabberwockybookshop.com

Tatnuck Bookseller
18 Lyman Street
Westborough MA 01581
Tel: 508-366-4959
Web: tatnuck.com

Odyssey Bookshop
9 College Street
South Hadley MA 01075
Tel: 413-534-7307
Web: odysseybks.com

Chapter Three

Bookstores in Massachusetts (Part II)
(Featuring Cape Cod Booksellers)

My favorite full-service bookstores on Cape Cod are:
- *Books by the Sea - Osterville*
- *Brewster Book Store - Brewster*
- *Main Street Books - Orleans*
- *Titcomb's Bookshop - East Sandwich*
- *Where the Sidewalk Ends - Chatham*

Books by the Sea

The curious thing about *Books by the Sea* in Osterville is that I used to shop at its annex in the Pondside Gift Shop in South Yarmouth more often than the main store. But, Pondside

Gifts is closed now, so when I want to browse the signed book section, it's off to Osterville.

I should point out that it's Osterville – and not Oysterville, which, survives as a silly running gag in our family.

Books by the Sea – Osterville

Open year round, they hold Author signings regularly and feature local writers as well as nationally recognized literati. The shop was established and continues to operate under the guidance of dedicated bibliophiles. They have a true interest in the books, writers, and those who seek good books and writing.

15

Brewster Bookstore

The town of Brewster is between Dennis and Orleans along Cape Cod Bay. Route 6 brings you quickly from the bridges East toward what some may characterize as a quintecential Cape Cod village, and the *Brewster Bookstore* serves in the role of quintecential community book shop. It's a full-service shop, open all year, with a rich history of being an important part of the local community.

Brewster Bookstore - Brewster

It appears to be a small shop, but it has 50,000 volumes on hand, which rates well for a community bookstore. During the summer season it held book signings on a weekly basis, from first-time writers to well-known featured Authors. My particular interest is with the extensive number of books about Cape Cod, both for adults and children, as well as the books written by local authors. All of this makes it more fun when you're vacationing to include the Brewster Bookstore for memorabilia of your trip and things to enhance your visit to Cape Cod.

Main Street Books

First, we stop for some clams, and then we head out for the bookstore. Maybe it's a coincidence that we are hungry when we get to Orleans, or maybe it's that the clams demand attention regardless of the time of day. But, with several excellent clam shacks, the Orleans area is often a destination for us.

16

At *Main Street Books*, I find that I agree with the owners that real books require paper, ink and a cover. While eBooks are here to stay, that doesn't mean the real book is gone forever. In fact, I am of the opinion that books – and thus

Main Street Books – Orleans

bookstores – are here forever. They may evolve, but they will be with us. I try to use a local bookstore to place my online orders, when it's not possible to find the book on hand. By using the services of the book shop I hope to be contributing to its survival. I don't want to price them into oblivion.

If we make our bookstore the conduit for books, instead of going direct through Amazon, for example, it increases the chance the local shop will be there for the things Amazon will never be. I can't imagine meeting Amazon's pet cat; or discussing whether a certain children's book is appropriate for my grandson.

Titcomb's Bookshop

Since 1974 *Titcomb's Book Shop* in East Sandwich has had a wrought iron colonial man statue on its lawn greeting visitors to the shop. Due to an unfortunate accident, where it was run down by a driver that got too close to the statue, a replacement colonial man was installed in 2011. Many famous Authors have posed with the statue over the years and you can see them on a wall of honor at the shop.

The bookstore offers new books, used books and author signings year round. The store has as many used books as you

17

might find in a used-book-only shop. I tend to run right up the stairs to begin my search for used books, but the main floor and the lower level are all well labeled and offer a lot of choices.

Titcomb's Bookshop – E.Sandwich

The shop's location on Route 6 is ideal for my frequent trips onto the Cape. I can either stop on my way onto the Cape or stop on my way off. Generally, I do both. Normally, I remember books I buy at various shops, but in this case I remember one I didn't buy. I was holding a copy of *Hitman* by Howie Carr, and for some reason I didn't buy – even though it was a signed copy. Howie had a book signing at Titcomb's. I got the book later, somewhere, without the signature because I was ready to read it. I should have bought it when I had it in my hand.

Where the Sidewalk Ends Bookstore

Every year we make it a point to do some of our Christmas shopping in Chatham. The off-season visit to Cape Cod is part of our whole approach to visiting this glacial-induced sandbar. To make the leisurely pace even more comfortable, I like to pick up a book at *Where the Sidewalk Ends* on Main Street.

The Christmas Stroll in Chatham seems to circulate in, around, through and about Where the Sidewalk Ends. From signed copies of local author's books to a large children's section, perfect for gift ideas, the bookstore

Where the Sidewalk Ends – Chatham

18

is always a treat. Even though we are off-Capers (not locals), we feel like family during the holiday stretch between Halloween and New Year's. I tend to favor non-fiction including biographies, memoirs of the famous and infamous and anything by Stephen Ambrose. But, that's me.

The quaint shop is well stocked and its recent addition of a children's annex has expanded its floor space. The local author and regional interest table dominates the central area with an imaginative collection of books to consider. There is a small second floor with more books and frequently a cart is placed near the front entrance with today's bargains. They go quick, and you never know what may be offered next. The summer visitor to the Cape can count on in-store events as well as more elaborate author events held off-site.

We haven't yet been there for the First Night celebration, but it's my guess that the festive nature of the Chatham locals, the non-Capers that are adding this location to the vacation destinations and the spirit you find at Where the Sidewalk Ends will make this a good bet for your next visit.

Books by the Sea
846 Main Street
Osterville MA 02655
Tel: 508-420-9400
Web: booksbythesea.net

Brewster Bookstore
2648 Main Street
Brewster MA 02631
Tel: 508-896-6543
Web: brewsterbookstore.com

Main Street Books
46 Main Street
Orleans MA
Tel: 508-255-3343
Web: mainstreetbookstore.com

Titcomb's Bookshop
423 Massachusetts Avenue
East Sandwich MA 02537
Tel: 508-888-2331
Web: titcombsbookshop.com

Where the Sidewalk Ends Bookstore
432 Main Street
Chatham MA 02633
Tel: 508-945-0499
Web: booksonthecape.com

Chapter Four

Bookstores in New Hampshire

My favorite full-service bookstores in New Hampshire are:
- *Country Bookseller – Wolfeboro*
- *River Run Bookstore – Portsmouth*
- *Toadstool Bookshop – Peterborough*
- *Village Bookstore – Littleton*
- *White Birch Books – North Conway*

Of all the six New England states, I probably have spent more vacation time in New Hampshire than any other. Some of my earliest memories are of family adventures in the Lakes Region and the White Mountains. For many years, my brother and I attended camp, for the entire summer, in Rumney Depot, which is right next to Rumney NH. Go figure.

My brother liked Ruggles Mine and I liked the Polar Caves. And today, they are both still attracting tourists. For many years my Dad, my brother and I hiked the Appalachian Trail, with the ultimate goal of joining the White Mountain 4,000 footer Club. We didn't achieve the status of climbing all 48 peaks to earn top honors, but we climbed a lot of them over the years.

We also spent summer vacations at Lake Winnipesaukee and Newfound Lake. For many years my Father kept a boat on Winnipesaukee at Gilford Marina. Motorcycle weekend was something that always stood out in my memory. Even today, we spend a lot of time visiting these areas and some of my favorite bookstores are right here.

21

Country Bookseller

The *Country Bookseller* in Wolfeboro is set back from the street in what was once the Durgin Stables. There is a penny candy shop and other stores in the small mall-like building. The book shop also houses a café for such things as muffins, cookies and coffee. I like to enter a bookshop and smell the baked goods. Why does that make me want to read? Not sure.

Country Bookseller - Wolfeboro

They have a good children's book section, which is always important to me, as it's a helpful way to introduce books and reading to grandchildren, nieces, and nephews. When they get books on vacation, it seems like it's supposed to be fun.

River Run Bookstore

In Portsmouth, the first place I stop when I get to town is the *River Run Bookstore*. I'm sorry that it's used book shop has been closed, but maybe it will reappear in the future. The shop has undergone a refurbishment and it looks great. Also great is the practice of putting new and used books together on the same shelf, so I can find bargains in every category. This feature is something I applaud when I find it.

River Run Bookstore -Portsmouth

Another thing at River Run is the sale feature where if you buy two used books, you get a third one free. The total cost for the three books allows them to compete directly with the online sources that also have to charge for shipping. If you can walk in and buy three books, you will have more fun, get a better deal and help keep the local store on its feet.

Toadstool Bookshop

There are three Toadstool Bookshops in Southern New Hampshire, which I visit regularly. The *Toadstool Bookshop* in Peterborough NH is one of my favorite book shops, but so are its

sister operations in Keene and Milford NH. I may have selected Peterborough, because we like to ride up to Mount Monadnock and it's the convenient stop when we do. But, the other two Toadstools are excellent as well.

Toadstool Bookshop – Peterborough

The Peterborough Toadstool is a part of the Depot Square area, which features an array of quaint shops and great places for food and drink. It's a great destination for locals on any Sunday afternoon, and anytime for vacationers. In fact, you can even get something to eat inside the bookstore. Now, that's convenient.

The Toadstool shops offer full-service, including a wide choice of children's books, local authors and a lot of community activities including poetry readings. I especially like the amount of used books offered at all locations. There are times at the Keene location where the cart has free books. That's about as low price as you can get.

I attended a book signing at Keene where the two local authors told the behind the scenes story about the book they had

23

written together as a sort of history project about the local airport. It was an overflow crowd of locals supporting the writers, the store and the community. It was well worth the effort to attend.

Village Bookstore

In Littleton, the *Village Bookstore* is my source for books about New Hampshire. They carry *the 4,000 Footer of the White Mountain* guide book, which is perfect to help me remember the climbs I made – and the one's I didn't.
Since those early days climbing with my Father through the White Mountains, my visits have been at quaint inns, luxurious resorts, and not the huts of the Appalachian trails or the Lodge on Mt. Moosilaukee. But, the long-time owners of the Village

Village Bookstore – Littleton

Bookstore feature books such as *The Moosilaukee Reader*, which sparked memories of the many times we hiked this peak and the views from the top of old "baldy." Moosilaukee is a Native American term that roughly means hill that is bare on top. Old Baldy.

The shop features a café and a special dedication to children's book and toys. It's important when on vacation to have a source of amusements for the little ones and the selection here is excellent.

White Birch Books

When we travel in New Hampshire, we probably stop in North Conway, even when our destination doesn't require it. We like the whole town, from the train to the kitschy gift shops. When they put up the Snow Men on the sidewalks, we can't help taking pictures. Why else would they put them there?

White Birch Books – No.Conway

White Birch Books is at one end of the main drag of North Conway and serves as a great kick-off to our visits. I always find some good bargains on the library cart. The owners work hard to feature local authors, including book signings and prominent displays to showcase their work. The shop has a great section for children's books and if they don't have it they are happy to order it for you.

Country Bookseller
23 North Main Street
Wolfeboro NH 03894
Tel: 603-569-6030
Web: thecountrybookseller.com

River Run Bookstore
142 Fleet Street
Portsmouth NH 03801
Tel: 603-431-2100
Web: riverrunbookstore.com

Toadstool Bookshop
12 Depot Street
Peterborough NH 03458
Tel: 603-924-3543
Web: toadbooks.com

Village Bookstore
81 Main Street
Littleton NH 03561
Tel: 603-444-5263
Web: booksmusictoys.com

White Birch Books
2568 Main Street
North Conway NH 03818
Tel: 603-356-3200
Web: whitebirchbooks.com

Chapter Five

Bookstores in Rhode Island

My favorite full-service bookstores in Rhode Island are:
- *Barrington Books – Barrington*
- *Island Books – Middletown*
- *Other Tiger – Westerly*
- *Wakefield Books – Wakefield*

In the spirit of full disclosure, I should admit that I was born in Rhode Island. And, after college, my first paying job was in Rhode Island. That said, I have spent a lot more time not in Rhode Island than in it, but, I go back as often as I can. Partly because it's my birthplace, but, there are a lot of better reasons than that. First, it's truly the Ocean State. From Westerly to Newport, it's a place that offers a lot of coastal attractions for vacationers.

Barrington Books
Some more history: My parents met at college in Barrington RI. That's why I was born in RI. As a family we developed a lot of local friends in RI and that continues today. But, for our purpose in this visitor Guide, the book shops mentioned get no special treatment from me. They are great and worth your visit regardless of my prejudice for all things Ocean State.

Barrington Books – Barrington

27

Barrington Books continues to earn local kudos for its wide selection, it's commitment to the community and it's highly regarded children's story hour held every week. On Thursday mornings, a reader leads the children into discovering several theme-related stories and picture books. This is followed by craft time and all at no cost to the participants.

Island Books

For nearly 20 years, *Island Books* in Middletown has been operating as a full-service independent book shop. It's a shop where there are booksellers that actually know about books. If your taste runs to biographies and history, they are able to find what you need. The book shop draws its name from Aquidneck Island, which is where Middletown resides.

Island Books – Middletown

The staff devotes a lot of effort to showcasing local books and local authors. For those vacationing in the area, there are many book choices to help you enjoy your visit, ranging from guides to the Newport Mansions to how to understand a Rhode Islander's accent. There is also a wide selection of children's books, which no vacation can survive without.

Other Tiger

The *Other Tiger* book shop is a testament to local owners respecting the needs of its readers. They go out of their way to help local, self-published authors to find readers that might never find the books otherwise in the big box stores or even online. We have reached a point where traditional book publishers, online publishing, and self-publishing must all be embraced as part of the whole and not as enemies. By the way, I view their offer to pay you for a used Kindle (so they can smash it) as an art project and not as skirmish in the publishing wars.

Other Tiger – Westerly

Wakefield Books

It's probably a bit immature for me to take some glee at seeing the *Wakefield Books* take over for the big box chain book store that failed. But, what the heck; they started this war and I'm taking some comfort in seeing a small town in Rhode Island (my home state) win one for the independent bookstore users.

Wakefield Mall – Home of
Wakefield Books – Wakefield

While it's not quaint, rural, or even slightly kitschy like the places that you find throughout most of this Guide, Wakefield Books is still the type of shop we must continue to support if the community is to come first and the interests of international business giants is to come second. So, congratulations to the folks in Wakefield for their courage in stepping up and making this happen.

29

Barrington Books
184 Country Road
Barrington RI 02806
Tel: 401-245-7925
Web: barringtonbooks.com

Island Books
575 East Main Road
Middletown RI 02842
Tel: 401-849-2665
Web: islandbooksri.com

Other Tiger
90 High Street
Westerly RI 02891
Tel: 401-596-2200
Web: othertiger.com

Wakefield Books
160 Old Tower Hill Road
Wakefield RI 02879
Tel: 401-792-0000
Web: wwakefieldbooks.com

Chapter Six

Bookstores in Vermont (Northern)

My favorite full-service bookstores in Vermont are:
- *Bear Pond Books – Montpelier*
- *Boxcar and Caboose Bookstore – St. Johnsbury*
- *Crow Bookshop – Burlington*
- *Galaxy Bookshop – Hardwick*
- *Phoenix Books – Essex*
- *The Vermont Book Shop – Middlebury*

Vacationers will find plenty of great book shops in Vermont, so many in fact, that I have split the state in half. Some folks split the state East/West; others into four quarters, and still others dice it up like a baked pie on the window sill. I have tried to present the two sections in a manner that is most helpful for planning visits while on vacation.

As this edition of the Guide went to press, the *Briggs Carriage Bookstore* in Brandon turned up closed. We stopped to visit and found an empty storefront. The ice cream shop next door consoled us a bit, but it still hurts to see a shop close down.

Our vacations range from golf adventures near Smuggler's Notch or Killington (we're not skiers) to cozy bed and breakfasts near Woodstock or somewhere in the Northeast Kingdom. Everywhere we go we learn about new things and places to come back for another time. That's why I have visited so many book shops.

Bear Pond Books

For nearly 40 years, *Bear Pond Books* has been a staple in downtown Montpelier, surviving vandalism and flooding, thanks to the support of local citizens. When the community book shop puts the community first, the feeling is mutual.

Bear Pond Books – Montpelier

The store features lots of books about Vermont and books by Vermont authors. But, they recognize that the times are a changing and you can turn to their website for the eBooks you need as well. And speaking as a writer, they have a generous attitude toward the newly published, including self-published authors, who can place books on consignment in the shop. This helps budding authors get a foothold in a very competitive marketplace.

Boxcar and Caboose

The town of St. Johnsbury is labeled as the gateway to the northern kingdom and I can't dispute that description. The area is beautiful and always worth the trip. *The Boxcar and Caboose* bookshop and café is the icing on the cake for a bibliophile. It's an inviting stop when traveling through Northern Vermont.

Boxcar and Caboose – St. Johnsbury

They have cleverly tied the café to the store by offering discounts on books based on your purchases in the café. And if

32

you are truly happy about your experience, you can write your own book and they will publish it for you on their own print-on-demand machine. Now, that's full service.

Crow Bookshop

When you read as many books as I do, and when you have a pastime of collecting books, the budget always comes to mind. At the *Crow Bookshop* in Burlington, the 20 percent off all the time on hard cover books is a big help. I sometimes have to buy a new book and it's helpful to find

Crow Bookshop – Burlington

someone who discounts right at the top of the reader pile. They also support the used book buyer, including a plan to earn credits when you turn in books, toward purchase of more used books. I like that too.

When we stop at the Church Street area in Burlington it seems we can't visit everywhere we want to go. There is so much to see and do. But, the book shop is worth seeking out at the far end of Church Street. Don't miss it.

Galaxy Bookshop

Sometimes the best move is one that consolidates all that's good and reduces what is bad. The move of the *Galaxy Bookshop* from its location on Mill Street to its new location on Main Street

Galaxy Bookshop – Hardwick
(Old Location)

33

gives the shop less room, more foot traffic, and probably reduced costs, so it can operate more efficiently. I have seen other shops move to smaller places, such as Toadstool Bookshop in Keene NH to its advantage. Smaller may be better.

The shop was pretty good to begin with. For more than 20 years the independent shop has been a fixture in the area.

Phoenix Books

Elsewhere in this Guide I express some glee that a local independent bookstore has opened where the big box used to be. And for *Phoenix Books* of Essex it's great also to see it expand into a second bookstore in Burlington.

Phoenix Books – Essex

This is all to the good. The local independent book shop owner is focused on meeting the needs of local customers (and an occasional tourist like me) and therefore makes decisions that help, rather than diminish, the local economy. The Phoenix Books location in Essex has been there for about five years. With this expansion, the owners continue to make a commitment despite the pressures of eBooks, Amazon, and the remaining big box outlets.

The Vermont Book Shop

Middlebury is the kind of place where I can conduct a *One-Day Bookstore-Tour* without leaving the town. It's similar in that manner to Woodstock, where I can do the same thing. Since 2007 the most recent owners of *The Vermont Book Shop* have devoted a lot of time and effort to improving the building, the

34

displays and the collection in a manner that reflects well on the independent book shop. The shop devotes a lot of space to Vermont-themed books and authors, which is what I'm looking for as a tourist. The photo books, the

The Vermont Book Shop – Middlebury

local tales told in verse and prose are what make this shop special. They claim to have been Robert Frost's favorite bookshop and I can see why.

Bear Pond Books
77 Main Street
Montpelier VT 05602
Tel: 802-229-0774
Web: bearpondbooks.com

Boxcar and Caboose Bookstore
394 Railroad Street
Saint Johnsbury VT 05819
Tel: 802-748-3551
Web: boxcarandcaboose.com

Crow Bookshop
14 Church Street
Burlington VT 05401
Tel: 802-862-0848
Web: crowbooks.com

Galaxy Bookshop
41 South Main Street
Hardwick VT 05843
Tel: 802-472-5533
Web: crowbooks.com

Phoenix Books
21 Essex Way
Essex Junction VT 05452
Tel: 802-872-7111
Web: phoenixbooks.biz

The Vermont Book Shop
38 Main Street
Middlebury VT 05753
Tel: 802-388-2061
Web: vermontbookshop.com

Chapter Six

Bookstores in Vermont (Southern)

My favorite full-service bookstores in Vermont are:
- *Book King Books – Rutland*
- *Misty Valley Books – Chester*
- *Northshire Bookstore – Manchester Center*
- *Shiretown Books – Woodstock*
- *Village Square Booksellers – Bellows Falls*
- *Yankee Bookshop – Woodstock*

Since I published the first edition of the Guide I have been back to Central and Southern Vermont so many times it seems impossible that I would not have visited every bookstore in the state. But, that's not true. As recently as 2012 I found shops I had never been to before. Even the visitors to my website have not given me enough leads as to where they all are. And, what's better, some new shops are opening, despite others having to close. So, it's important to pay attention to the local bookstores and keep them viable.

A recent golf vacation headquartered in Rutland opened my eyes to a beautiful shop right downtown. The Book King moved to Center Street three years ago into the historic Tuttle building. When I walked in and saw the woodwork and the expansive layout, it was very impressive. Once I lowered my eyes and began to look at the books, I was even more impressed. Read more about the shop in the Guide descriptions.

Book King Books

We went downtown to find a particular restaurant and my eyes landed on the *Book King Books* sign. So we checked to see if it was open – it wasn't, but I set my sights on coming back later. I'm glad we did. The shelves were as impressive as the books. I like a display that provides enough room to see everything without having to assume awkward positions. The table top displays, the well-lighted sections make all of this easy.

Book King Books – Rutland

I also enjoyed the balcony. It's a cozy place to read and it's the best way to enjoy the ultra-high ceilings with the windows overlooking the street. The shop features local authors and holds regular book signings. There is a large collection of local authors and books about the region to satisfy anyone.

Misty Valley Books

The current owners have been operating the shop for more than a decade and in that time it has continued to be a destination bookstore for many people. Authors go out of their way – and in this case, way out of their way, to make an appearance in Chester, Vermont. I take pictures of the shops I visit to share on my website and my blog, but this is one of the shops

Misty Valley Books – Chester

where I take a picture every time I visit. It's always picturesque, and with the quaint neighbor buildings and the town green outside, it's no wonder that it's so popular.

But, things like the color-coordinated display table are more about what the shop is like. On a recent visit the display table featured all green books. Book covers were green, or the image on the cover was green, or the subject of the book was green. It's a regular feature for the display to reflect the color of the season. Yellow for spring, Green for summer; and you can imagine the rest. It turns out that this practice helps sell books. That's what I like to hear.

Northshire Bookstore

Right in the middle of the Green Mountain National Forest, at what sort of serves as the crossroads of Rt 7, Rt 7A, Rt 30, and Rt 11 is the *Northshire Bookstore*, dominating its downtown location now for more than 30 years. The shop has evolved over the years to expand its floor space, add a café, and has even become a source for self-publishing.

Northshire Bookstore – Manchester

Customers will drive a long way to reach this destination, and it's worth it. The children's section is large, they have all the newest books on hand and there are bargains to be had if you are willing to browse aggressively.

They have embraced the electronic age with an active blog that offers nearly daily updates covering reviews of books by several different reviewers. They offer books online and will print books with their on demand equipment if you have a short-run book you want to print.

Shiretown Books

The last time I was in Woodstock, I got a parking ticket in front of *Shiretown Books* at a meter on Central Street. It happens to me from time to time when I get distracted and spend too much time in a shop. In Woodstock, I was trying to visit two shops on one meter and I blew it. But, when I filled out the form and walked over to the bin where you drop your ticket and your payment at the

Shiretown Books – Woodstock

sidewalk container, the meter guy started to write up another ticket! I ran back across the street and showed him I was trying to pay the first one, which he wrote about five minutes earlier. He said I should have moved the car. I said, "To where should I move it?" There were no spaces from here to Chester. Anyway, he waived the second ticket once he saw I had already paid the first. Warning: don't get too distracted at Shiretown or Yankee Bookshop across the street.

Village Square Booksellers

On the border between Vermont and New Hampshire is the *Village Square Booksellers* in Bellows Falls. This shop has been around for more than 20 years, under the current ownership for about a dozen. The shop has a good offering including a strong children's section. A lot of attention is paid to local Authors

40

from both states and you can find signed copies of their books in the shop.

Village Square Booksellers – Bellows Falls

As we drive up from Massachusetts, I always seem to make the left turn at Bellows Falls as my entry into Vermont. I've had more than enough of the big highway and I want to seek out the by-ways and back roads. It's the gateway to Chester, Rutland, and Manchester. All places with lots of books calling to me.

Yankee Bookshop

Make sure you have enough money in the meter outside so you can take your time browsing at The *Yankee Bookshop* in Woodstock. (See related story at Shiretown listing). Since 1935 the shop has graced the quaint downtown of Woodstock. The shop is just steps from Bentley's Restaurant

Yankee Bookshop – Woodstock

and the Red Rooster at the Woodstock Inn, two of my favorite haunts in Woodstock. The cocktails are great at both, but cheaper at Bentley's.

The bookshop advertises itself as the oldest continuously operated independent bookstore in the area. In addition to all of the latest best sellers, they offer an expanded collection of books you might not expect to find in a general purpose shop.

Book King Books
11 Center Street
Rutland VT 05701
Tel: 802-202-4465
Web: bookkingbooks.com

Misty Valley Books
58 Common Street
Chester VT 05143
Tel: 802-875-3400
Web: mvbooks.com

Northshire Bookstore
4869 Main Street
Manchester Center VT 05255
Tel: 802-362-2200
Web: northshire.com

Shiretown Books
9 Central Street
Woodstock VT 05091
Tel: 802-457-2996
Web: shiretownbooks.com

Village Square Booksellers
32 The Square
Bellows Falls VT 05101
Tel: 802-463-9404
Web: villagesquarebooks.com

Yankee Bookshop
12 Central Street
Woodstock VT 05091
Tel: 802-457-2411
Web: yankeebookshop.com

USED/RARE BOOK SHOPS

My interest in books, book shops, bookstores, booksellers, book writing; and if you asked my wife, book shelves, keeps me pretty busy. I like to write, to read and to consider books in many ways. Perhaps more than a good independent, full-service bookstore, my strongest interest is in the used book shop.

Wherever I go, I seek out the used, rare and antiquarian bookshop. It's always fun to find one I've never been to before to see how it compares with my favorites. One of my handiest book shop guides that I've carried for years listed over 700 used book shops in New England. Many of them were not open shops, that is, you couldn't visit them, but nonetheless, the owners were willing to make an appointment to let you into their attic, cellar or barn to see the used, rare and antiquarian treasures they had collected.

As a result, my list of favorite book shops keeps changing. As one book shop closes, another opens; or merges with another. Each shop, as represented by the proprietor, reflects the region, the history, and the times we live in. I find them all fascinating and I am sharing my 31 favorites with you in this section of the Guide.

The Book Shed – Benson VT

Chapter Seven

Used Book Shops in Connecticut

My favorite used bookstores in Connecticut are:
- *Book Barn – Niantic*
- *Harbor Books – Old Saybrook*
- *Traveler Book Cellar – Union*
- *Whitlock Farm Booksellers – Bethany*

Used books are my not-so-secret passion. I talk about used books all the time because once I realized how much I could save by buying a used book it released me from my concern about over spending. I simply can't afford to pay for a NY Times best seller every week. But, I like to read a book or two a week. So what to do? Simple: lower the cost of entry through used books.

A friend said to me once, "Why not borrow from the library if cost is a concern?" My answer was, "I do borrow from the library, but I am also a collector and the library hates it when I don't return the books."

In the other part of this Guide where I describe my One-Day Bookstore-Tours, you will see that I visit a mix of new books and used book shops on these trips. That only makes sense, as I often find shops in close proximity to each other. There is a lot of natural co-existence ethic among and between shops, even when there are multiple shops on the same street. Each often has a specialty that anchors its claim to fame.

Book Barn

The *Book Barn* in Niantic has outgrown itself twice and so now occupies three separate locations to accommodate its nearly 500,000 volumes. The fun part is to watch the lineup of customers, each taking a number, who then form up to sell their books. Meanwhile, I am meandering the grounds moving from one small building to the next looking for bargains; wondering if the guy in line to sell his books has something I need. I guess I'll just have to wait. The woman

Niantic Book Barn – Niantic

with the "Number One" card was practically dancing in the aisle, in anticipation of selling her books when the "Sell Desk" opened at 11:00 a.m.

I've mentioned it before, but I generally try to get to their annual sale because it seems to me they make an effort to bring in more books for the sale, rather than just unload things that are moving slowly. It's just a guess, but it seems there are more choices than usual with books overflowing onto the floor where they haven't had time to get them up onto the shelves.

Harbor Books

In Old Saybrook, *Harbor Books* has a small, but eclectic collection of used and rare books. The owner is known for his interest in Katherine Hepburn, so you can expect a lot of various books about and by her. I have picked up some myself. I have also picked up some great military history books as well.

46

My interest in military biography was peaked when I found a copy of *Rickover: Controversy and Genius* by Thomas B. Allen and Norman Polmar. This book may have been the heaviest book I have ever bought, that wasn't a two-volume set. Pound per pound it was the day's best bargain.

Harbor Books – Old Saybrook

Traveler Book Cellar

The *Traveler Book Cellar* in Union is just over the Massachusetts border where you pick up I-84 off of the Mass. Turnpike to head south to New York. It's earned a bit of fame for its unusual practice of serving each meal in its café with a free book. In fact, each customer may take up to three books, per person, per table. My wife has actually taken some

Traveler Book Cellar – Union

free books, but, even though I enjoy the food and the atmosphere, I prefer to go downstairs and buy some books from the Book Cellar. The collection is small but the layout of the store is tidy. The chart of aisles at the foot of the stairs makes it easy to browse efficiently, and for those looking for signed copies of used books, they are gathered together in the same section.

Whitlock Farm Booksellers

Whitlock Farm Booksellers (also known as Whitlock's Book Barn) in Bethany is not very far from New Haven, which explains why you see a lot of used books written by Yale Law professors. But, that's exactly the benefit of visiting a rare book shop near such a college, because the natural drift of used books starts with the closest book shop. Eventually, you can find the book in Calcutta, but today, it's only a few miles from campus. There are two barns, one of which is self-service, that is, pick out a book and bring it to the other barn to pay for it.

Whitlock Farm Booksellers – Bethany

My wife has tuned in so well on my interests that the best find during a recent visit was a book she spotted on the window sill: *First World Flight, the Odyssey of Billy Mitchell,* by Spencer Lane. It was signed, included letters written and signed by Lane, including copies of newspaper articles and promotional flyers about the book's publication. I thought I knew a lot about Billy Mitchell, based on all my reading, but this book took me places I never knew about.

Book Barn
41 West Main Street
Niantic CT 06357
Tel: 860-739-5715
Web: bookbarnniantic.com
Book Barn Downtown – 269 Main Street
Book Barn Midtown – 291 Main Street

Harbor Books
146 Main Street
Old Saybrook CT 06475
Tel: 860-338-6850
Web: harborbooks.com

Traveler Book Cellar
1257 Buckley Highway
Union CT 06076
Tel: 860-684-9042
Use this Link to Yankee Magazine to read about the Book Cellar:
http://www.yankeemagazine.com/issues/2011-03/food/traveler-food-books

Whitlock Farm Booksellers (Whitlock's Book Barn)
20 Sperry Road
Bethany CT 06524
Tel: 203-393-1240
Web: whitlocksbookbarn

Chapter Eight

Used Book Shops in Maine

My favorite used bookstores in Maine are:
- *Bar Harbor Bookshop – Hulls Cove*
- *Big Chicken Barn Bookshop – Ellsworth*
- *Carlson Turner Books – Portland*
- *Harding's Books – Wells*

It's seems much easier to find a used book shop than a new book shop in Maine. Or, at least, that appears to be the case from my experience. A quick look at the Antiquarian Booksellers membership list shows over 50 subscribers. That's a lot of used books.

Bar Harbor Book Shop

The *Bar Harbor Book Shop* used to be known as Mystery Cove Bookshop. It's been the only used books shop in the Bar Harbor area for the past five years. It's easy to miss when you zip down Route 3 out of Bar Harbor into Hulls Cove. I have missed the turn more than once. But, once you find it, it's worth the trip. The shop is small and made to feel smaller because it's a house with books

Bar Harbor Bookshop – Hulls Cove

scattered in the different rooms. But, once you get a feel for it, it works well.

51

The signed book I bought the last time is one of the reasons I like this shop. I read a lot, but I also collect books of certain authors. And I always find something here.

Big Chicken Barn Bookshop

At the *Big Chicken Barn Bookshop* the experience is totally different. This place is so big that it defies description. With 150,000 books strewn out on the second floor of this former chicken barn it's hard to imagine anyone can get a feel for it in just one visit. I bought Tom Brokaw's *The Greatest Generation* and I even had my

Big Chicken Barn Bookshop - Ellsworth

choice of three copies; each at a different price point, obviously influenced by the wear and tear on the book.

If you want a "reader" to toss out or pass along when you are done, you could get it for a couple dollars. For a few dollars more, it could go on your shelf and look okay. And, then if you want the best choice, pay for the signed copy. That's a nice scenario for a book collector.

Carlson Turner Books

When you get to serious book collecting, you might want to try *Carlson Turner Books* in Portland, ME. With over 40,000 volumes, my interest in history, travel, and nautical is well covered. They have books about the Civil War, World War II and other military eras including biographies of military leaders and historical studies by well-known historians.

The shop is also a bindery, so if you have books that need repair, this is the place to go. They can restore a book in a manner that doesn't diminish its value as a collectible. That's important if you have made a significant investment.

Carlson Turner Books – Portland

It's possible that some readers may feel Portland is not part of the "rural" genre that I like to write about. And that may be true. But I view Portland differently than most "cities" along the New England coast. It's certainly not like Boston or Providence. For me, the City of Portland presents more like a large town rather than a big City.

Harding's Books

With 100,000 volumes on hand, including things I like such as Americana and maritime books, *Harding's Books* is a definite stop when visiting Maine. The shop moved to its current address in Wells about 30 years ago.

It was originally founded in 1960 in New Hampshire as a rare, antiquarian and out-of-print book shop. That emphasis continues

Harding's Books – Wells

today, but it has expanded to include a broad range of categories including fiction, literature, biographies and other categories.

53

Bar Harbor Book Shop
One Dewey Street
Hulls Cove ME 04644
Tel: 207-288-4665
Web: barharborbookshop.com

Big Chicken Barn Bookshop
1768 Bucksport Road
Ellsworth ME 04605
Tel: 207-667-7308
Web: bigchickenbarn.com

Carlson Turner Books
241 Congress Street
Portland ME 04101
Tel: 207-773-4200
Web: carlsonturnerbooks.com

Harding's Books
2152 Post Road
Wells ME 04090
Tel: 207-646-8785
Web: hardingsbooks.com

Chapter Nine

Used Book Shops in Massachusetts (Part I)
(Not Including Cape Cod)

My favorite used bookstores in Massachusetts are:
- *Book Bear – West Brookfield*
- *Manchester-by-the-Book – Manchester-by-the-Sea*
- *Montague Bookmill – Montague*
- *Shire Bookshop – Franklin*
- *Toad Hall Bookstore* – Rockport*

This newest edition of the Guide more precisely divides the used and new bookstores to make it easier for those who want a full-service shop, versus those who are seeking the antiquarian aspects of book collecting. The used shops won't have the latest Stephen King thriller, although they will often have a section filled with his early works – and at very reasonable prices. Unless, it's signed, in which case, it's expensive. But, that's the used and antiquarian trade.

Again, I have had to make the concession of dividing a state into two parts; regular Massachusetts and irregular: Cape Cod. The Cape has a lot of bookshops and so I have given it a section of its own to assist the vacationer in the Bay State.

Book Bear

The carved wooden bear in front of the shop is always a bit unsettling when I approach. I'm not sure what the genesis is for this unusual sculpture, and I have never bothered to ask. Maybe I

55

don't want to know. Anyway, once you get inside the tall, narrow stacks are brimming with great used books. But, let me back up. When I first come in the front door there is generally a library cart out front with books for about $1 or $2. I drop my selections at the front counter and continue shopping. It's become a ritual.

The sections inside are well marked so that I can get to the Americana without having to ask for help, including the new arrivals shelf at the front. It's a good chance to get a bargain before someone else sees it. The aisle categorization narrows enough so that I can find books on the Civil War or books on Presidents. That's so convenient for hiking down the aisles. The sections extend to Religion, Psychology, Literature, and so on. It's very well organized.

Manchester-by-the-Book

Going to the North Shore is a regular thing for us. My wife Patti is a long time scuba diver and Gloucester and Rockport are definite destinations for us. So, on the way, or on the way back, *Manchester by the Book* is a definite destination for me. It can be a destination for Patti, depending on her need for a book that day. I buy for the future; she just buys for the moment.

Manchester-by-the-Book –
Located in Manchester-by-the-Sea

The shop has evolved over the years with the children's section getting some improvements. The shop attracts families to its crafts activities and helps make reading fun for kids. The store always feels like there are more books in it then shelves to accommodate them. But, that works to our advantage as the selection is broad and deep. I still can't get the image of 48 John Updike books stacked in one pile with a price tag of $1,000. This was right after Updike had died and it was an odd tribute to his memory. I'm still trying to bring my Updike collection into line. But, you can read more about it in the One-Day Bookstore-Tour section of the Guide.

Montague Bookmill

This bookstore is very close to home; in some ways, it's too close, which makes it too easy to drop other things I should be doing and head out to Montague. The region is beautifully rural, the ride is all back-roads, there is an excellent on-site café and the new arrivals always reveal something tempting.

Montague Bookmill – Montague

I sometimes remind my wife that the great Feng shui book that she owns came from the *Montague Bookmill*. She got so engrossed in it while waiting for me to shop, that she decided to have me buy it for her so she could finish it. Not that she follows the philosophy too closely, but she is an amateur student of interior design principals. So, good association between Feng shui and Montague allows me to shop more often.

57

The bargain table at the front, the quiet upstairs area with comfortable couches, chairs and tables allow folks to crank up the Wi-Fi, and the café downstairs make this a destination book shop. By the way, I saw a car rolling in front of me in my home town of Jefferson with a bumper sticker from Montague Bookmill that said "Books You Don't Need in a Place You Can't Find." It's a clever saying, but only partly right. It may be hard to find, but I do need those books.

Shire Bookshop

The sheer size of the collection is the first thing you notice about the *Shire Bookshop* in Franklin. They have over 100,000 books on their shelves. The aisles are long and the shelves are very tall. So tall, that you need ladders to see what's on the top rows. But, the labeling is pretty good and the owners are always ready to zero you in to the book sections if you need

Shire Bookshop – Franklin

help. For the past 30 years, the shop has specialized in out-of-print, collectible and used books of all types.

The owners also make you a cup of tea when you first walk through the door. That is not something that you expect, but it is surely appreciated. Also appreciated is the care with which they wrap each book in its own archival protective cover if it doesn't already have one. They care about the books they sell and they care that you get it in a condition that will sustain it.

58

Toad Hall Bookstore

I have a special fascination for spiral staircases. When I see one I want to climb it. After I climb it I realize that it's a very impractical design, especially if I am trying to carry a dozen books back down to the check-out counter. Anyway, I still like to see the spiral staircase even if I don't like walking down. The shop, since its founding 40 years ago, has always donated any profits it makes to non-profit environmental groups.

While that's not a reason alone to shop there, it's kind of nice to know that recycling books has another level of value. Now, for those of you who know the shop, it's really not a used book shop; it's basically a full-service

Toad Hall Bookstore – Rockport

bookshop. But, I buy so many used books here that I have included it in this section of the Guide. It's a great used book shop. Let's call it a hybrid.

Book Bear
80 West Main Street
West Brookfield MA 01585
Tel: 508-867-8705
Web: thebookbear.com

Manchester-by-the-Book
27 Union Street
Manchester-by-the-Sea MA 01970
Tel: 978-525-2929
Web: manchesterbythebook.com

Montague Bookmill
440 Greenfield Road
Montague MA 01351
Tel: 413-367-9206
Web: montaguebookmill.com

Shire Bookshop
305 Union Street
Franklin MA 02038
Tel: 508-528-5665
Web: shirebookshop.com

Toad Hall Bookstore
47 Main Street
Rockport MA 01966
Tel: 978-546-7323
Web: toadhallbooks.org

*(Toad Hall Bookstore is a full-service book shop, but this is my Guide and I wanted to include it here for its excellent offering of used books, so I did.)

Chapter Nine

Used Book Shops in Massachusetts (Part II)
(Featuring Cape Cod Booksellers)

My favorite used bookstores in Massachusetts are:
- *Herridge Books - Wellfleet*
- *Isaiah Thomas Books - Cotuit*
- *Reed Books – Harwich Port*
- *Parnassus Book Services – West Yarmouth*
- *Tim's Used Books - Provincetown*
- *Yellow Umbrella - Chatham*

This chapter is devoted to the used book shops on Cape Cod, most of which I visit on a regular basis. We always do our Christmas shopping in Chatham; we have an annual week's fall vacation dedicated to playing golf, and we visit during other seasons as well. I find the Cape draws a unique range of used and rare books to its various shops. That makes the browsing and collecting very productive.

Herridge Books
Don't let the modest appearance of the shop deceive you. *Herridge Books* is home to a very nice collection of used and rare books. On different visits I have managed to always find something I didn't see

Herridge Books - Wellfleet

61

before. Are they bringing up books from the basement? Or, are they taking in new books at a quick pace? It all works to my advantage in discovering books I need right now. Of course, that's more about me and my needs than about the way they merchandise their product.

Isaiah Thomas Books

The shop has been in business for over 40 years, starting originally in Worcester just about the time I left the city for 10 years. Coincidence? Then, sometime after my return to the city, the shop pulled up stakes and moved to the Cape. Coincidence?

Isaiah Thomas Books - Cotuit

Since that time, Isaiah Thomas Books, has been a credit to its namesake as it preserves the used and rare books of the region, the country and the world. The shop carries over 70,000 books on hand with an emphasis on local authors and history, plus first editions, and such categories as art, photography, and architecture.

Reed Books

On our golf vacations, we always include the courses in Harwich and Harwich Port. Wequassett resort has an outstanding course, and we also enjoy the Harwich Port Golf Club and Cranberry Valley Golf Course. These courses are all on a route that I take right past *Reed Books*. That means I can stop here as frequently as I like.

On one recent visit, the owner mentioned that he has an additional 25,000 volumes not on the shelves. I recognize that it is not easy to keep up with the flow of books in and out. I hope to get a closer look at those volumes during my next visit.

He also mentioned that the chef at Cranberry Valley was a bit above what you might expect at a local golf course, and he was right. My wife and I made it a point to have dinner there after we played golf, and we were not disappointed.

Reed Books – Harwich Port

Patti even liked the way the place was decorated. There is a lesson here for vacationers. The local shop owners know where the good stuff is; so don't hesitate to ask.

Parnassus Book Services

I still get a kick out of seeing the hundreds of books on the outside shelves at *Parnassus Book Services* in Yarmouth Port. It seems slightly outrageous to have the books outside, and to expect customers to select them and leave money behind on their own time. But, it's been that way for as long as I can remember.

Parnassus Book Services – Yarmouth Port

Sadly, we lost the founder of the shop, Ben Muse, this year. He will be truly missed by the community and his customers. I hope the shop will be able to continue with the tradition he established over these many years.

The books on the shelves had a certain order that you could follow, but the books on the floor were a bit more of a challenge.

63

But, someone was always available to guide me to where I could find what I needed; even if I didn't know I needed it.

Tim's Used Books

There are two locations for *Tim's Used Books* on Cape Cod. The one I'm listing is in Provincetown. The other is in Hyannis. I shop both. I got *War and Peace* in Hyannis just last year. But, the fun shop is the Tim's in Provincetown, where you have to "navigate off road" to quote my GPS. (Whenever you turn off a main road onto a golf course entrance or resort driveway, my GPS

Tim's Books - Provincetown

barks, "navigate off road," as if I was going to turn onto the tundra.)

But, in Provincetown, the house where Tim's resides is set way back from the road and sidewalk, which sets you up for the type of shop it is. The compact space is stuffed with used books, and a careful search always yields something that I just have to take with me. When you finally leave Provincetown, you can drive through Hyannis on your way off Cape and check out his second location.

Yellow Umbrella

Any stop in Chatham is not complete without lunch at the *Wild Goose Tavern* and high tea at the *Chatham Bars Inn*. It's also not complete without a stop at the *Yellow Umbrella* on Main Street. I consider this one of my favorite used book shops, even though you can find new books here too. It's a bit of a hybrid

64

shop. The used books are well sorted and the collection is deep enough that I always find something I like.

The shop has a bit of everything you need for a vacation purchase. They have some literary standards, a children's area, and books about the Cape or written by Cape Codders. There is also an emphasis on the nautical, which seems fitting given the setting at the elbow of Cape Cod.

Yellow Umbrella - Chatham

Books come and go so fast, that when I check out, whoever is ringing me up is likely to muse that they hadn't known my selection was on hand. (They may have grabbed it ahead of me.) The shop has been a fixture in Chatham for about 35 years and I'm sure it's going to be around for a long time.

Herridge Books
11 Main Street
Wellfleet MA 02667
Tel: 508-349-1323
Web: facebook.com/HerridgeBooks

Isaiah Thomas Books
4632 Falmouth Road
Cotuit MA 02635
Tel: 508-428-2785
Web: isaiahthomasbooks.com

Reed Books
559 Main Street
Harwich Port MA 02646
Tel: 508-432-5293
Web: facebook.com/pages/Reed-Books

Parnassus Book Services
220 Old Kings Highway
Yarmouthport MA 02675
Tel: 508-362-6420
Web: parnassusbooks.com

Tim's Used Books
242 Commercial Street
Provincetown MA 02657
Tel: 508-487-0005
Web: facebook/pages/Tims-Used-Books
    Hyannis – 386 Main Street

Yellow Umbrella
501 Main Street
Chatham MA 02633
Tel: 508-945-0144
Web: yellowumbrella.net

Chapter Ten

Used Book Shops in New Hampshire

My favorite used bookstores in New Hampshire are:
- *Drake Farm Books – North Hampton*
- *Henniker Book Farm – Henniker*
- *The Colophon Bookshop – Exeter*

It occurs to me that I may have to write a separate Guide for each New England state in order to cover the large number of fine used bookstores I have discovered. Those listed here are among my favorites, but there are actually many more.

The used bookshop varies from warehouse style to cramped attic or cellar. Some shops are lodged behind the owner's home and others occupy old mills or barns. Unlike the typical full-service independent bookstore, the shop may operate more irregularly than typical retail outlets, thus requiring vigilance in calling ahead before setting out to visit a used book store.

Where possible I have included websites, phone numbers and physical addresses to assist vacationers seeking to visit the used, as well as, the new book shops. But, especially with used shops, be sure to double-check before heading out. Also, check the antiquarian book association contact information at the back of the Guide for more help in finding the best used and antiquarian book shops.

Drake Farm Books

This big yellow barn is home to thousands of great books. The appearance at first may seem cluttered, but it's really just overstuffed with books. The aisles are labeled and shelves are labeled too. Many of the books are wrapped in plastic as they sit on the shelf. When you buy a book, there is some further discounting the more you spend.

Drake Farm Books – North Hampton

If you are interested in getting into the book selling business, this is one of the many shops currently for sale. In fact, much like boat owners, book sellers are generally open to offers to buy them out; even if it's so they can go ahead and buy or start another book shop.

On my last visit, an officer from the nearby naval base was browsing for nautical literature. That's the beauty of the used book shop. The out-of-print and rare book is sitting on a shelf somewhere, just waiting for you to come in and claim it. The officer left with several books he would never find in a regular bookstore. With 45,000 books on hand, there is something for everyone.

The barn dates from about 1830, which makes it a treat as an historical structure that still features heat from an antique railroad station wood stove. Sometimes that's the only heat in the building, particularly when customer traffic is slow and the owner turns off the conventional heating. You can limit your visits to warmer months, or plan on bringing some mittens.

Henniker Book Farm

The town of Henniker is the home to New England College, which is a private four-year liberal arts school, founded after WWII. *Henniker Book Farm* is only three miles from the college, about 20 minutes west of the capital city of Concord.

Henniker Book Farm – Henniker

The rural feel is complete when you are at the school and the bookstore, but a small taste of city life is right up the road. If you trace the roots of the shop back to its founder, you will find he was a college professor and the shop was started in his house. As the years went by, others bought the shop and managed to maintain what is now a 50 year legacy of service.

I don't generally do this, but I refer you to their website for its glossary of book terms. Things like "foxing" and "tipped in" were a bit of a mystery to me until I found this resource. Try it.

The Colophon Bookshop

My preferences are for biographies and other non-fiction accounts about the Revolutionary War, the Civil War, and World Wars I & II. *The Colophon Bookshop* has been a source for many of the books I have found

The Colophon Bookshop – Exeter

about the men, women, commanders, and nations at war. I visit often, but I also get their email letters and use their online services when I spot something I want right away. I don't think it's a violation of any code to help the independent bookstore through the Internet. It just may be that the combined direct hand-selling in the shop and the Internet income will keep them viable. I'm still waiting for the price on *Hitler's Pilot* by Lt. Gen. Hans Baur to come down so I can afford it. I'm patient.

Drake Farm Books
148 Lafayette Road
North Hampton NH 03862
Tel: 603-964-4868
Web: drakefarmbooks.com

Henniker Book Farm
34 Old West Hopkinton Road
Henniker NH 03242
Tel: 603-428-8888
Web: hennikerbookfarm.com

The Colophon Bookshop
101B Water Street
Exeter NH 03833
Tel: 603-772-8443
Web: colophonbooks.com

Chapter Eleven

Used Book Shops in Rhode Island

My favorite used bookstores in Rhode Island are:
- *All Booked Up – Coventry*
- *D. Kelley Fine Used Books – Newport*
- *Myopic Books – Providence*
- *Spring Street Books – Newport*

No visit to Rhode Island is complete without stopping off in Newport. Just the mansions alone are reason enough to visit. But, the deep sea fishing out of Newport for blues and tuna is something I won't forget. I won't forget the seasickness either, but I got over that. The holiday decorations at the Mansions are inspiring and spectacular. Other parts of Rhode Island are fun as well, and we use any excuse to visit.

While I am there, it's easy to find a great bookstore, and especially a used book store. Shops such as D. Kelley Fine Used Books are not to be missed.

All Booked Up

Offering over 30,000 used books, *All Booked Up* should have something you like. In operation for over a decade, it also sells puzzles and crafts. It's sometimes

All Booked Up – Coventry

important to spread your wings and offer more than just books if you want to remain competitive.

71

D. Kelley Fine Used Books

There are several shops that I frequent that have characteristics that I associate with the type of book shop I might like to own myself. When you enter *D. Kelley Fine Used Books* in Newport, the owner may not be out front. He

D. Kelley Fine Used Books – Newport

might be out back sorting books. That's what he's been doing since 1995 when he opened the shop. He won't come out to acknowledge you because he assumes you want to browse – or else, why would you be in an antiquarian and rare book shop anyway? Reed Books on Cape Cod or Pleasant Street Books in Woodstock VT are like that too.

At D. Kelley, they understand you want to see books, have them around, read them, collect them, display them, share them and then start over. D. Kelley is my kind of place. The shop does not currently have a website, so be sure to telephone for updates on shop hours.

Myopic Books

This is another example of a bookstore that benefits from its proximity to great colleges. The Rhode Island School of Design and Brown University are nearby to *Myopic Books*, and provide an eclectic run of student browsers

Myopic Books – Providence

to help keep this shop lively. The shop carries a wide selection of rare and used books for every taste. The shop is in the Wayland

72

Square neighborhood of Providence, so it's like being in a small town within a large city.

Although it appears small, the shop has about 20,000 books in its collection at any time, so you really do have a good selection to draw from. They feature art, architecture, philosophy and other areas you would expect in a college environment.

Spring Street Books

As I said, Newport is a frequent stop for us. We have spent weekends and occasionally, week-long vacations in this quaint port city. We have visited the mansions frequently, so some tour guides don't explain the headsets to us anymore because they recognize us. There are many shops in town including *Spring Street Books*, which features mostly used books, but some new books too. It's a bit unusual that they moved from exclusively online to a bricks and mortar store, instead of the reverse, which has been the case for many traditional shops that eventually adopted the online presence.

Spring Street runs between Bellevue and Thames. These two streets have all the action. Bellevue has the mansions and Thames runs along the water. Spring Street lies between them where I'm sure the rent is less. Good spot for a used book shop.

All Booked Up
799 Tiogue Avenue
Coventry RI 02816
Tel: 401-826-3700
Web: allbookedup-ri.com

D. Kelley Fine Used Books
330 Broadway
Newport RI 02840
Tel: 401-846-4140

Myopic Books
5 South Angell Street
Providence RI 02906
Tel: 401-521-5533
Web: myopicbooks.com

Spring Street Books
42 Spring Street
Newport RI 02840
Tel: 401-609-3323
Web: springstreetbooksri.com

Chapter Twelve

Used Book Shops in Vermont

My favorite used bookstores in Vermont are:
- *Hermit Hills – Poultney*
- *Pleasant Street Books – Woodstock*
- *Sandy's Books – Rochester*
- *The Book Shed – Benson*
- *The Country Bookshop – Plainfield*

Among my favorite used book shops in Vermont are shops such as Hermit Hills. This book shop is one of the four shops that got me started on the habit of One-Day Bookstore-Tours that I write about on my blog: Richard-Wright.Blogspot.com. When I saw the section on Joseph Trenn's website: *TheBookShed.com* about his One Day Bookstore Tour I was intrigued. Here was one bookstore talking about his competitors. But, if you look closely, he lists many book shop links on his website in support of their efforts to offer the rare, antiquarian and used book to the buying public.

If you visit his website, you will see that he describes a tour that includes Hermit Hills Books, The Book Shed, Bulwagga Books, and Seasoned Booksellers (now called Sandy's Books). It's a "scenic trip through Vermont's mountains and valleys – the perfect day trip for any time of year." I agree.

Hermit Hills

It's just a short hop to Green Mountain College from the *Hermit Hills* bookstore. The shop has 30,000 volumes and has been operating for the past 15 years. When I saw their claim to having "Vermontiana", I thought it was a play on Americana, which I like very much. But, they soon showed me that it's a serious specialty, with colleges and bookstores focusing a

Hermit Hills - Poultney

lot of interest on the post cards, maps, catalogs, railroad schedules, and you-name-it that came from Vermont.

The rest of the collection includes history, science, nature, and literature. They also feature modern first editions, which for collectors such as myself, is very important.

Pleasant Street Books

Someday I will write about all the book shops in a barn. It seems to me that it's a frequent occurrence for shops to spring up in sheds, lofts and barns. The rent is low and the space is open, which makes it ideal for aisles of books. *Pleasant Street Books* is in a quintessential horse/cow barn from years ago. It was converted about 25 years ago, which now makes it

Pleasant Street Books - Woodstock

comfortable and cozy, with plenty of chairs for sitting to review a book. There are small stools to sit on upstairs when you are straining to read the spines on books on the lower shelves. And there is plenty of light too.

Sonny Saul told me that he rearranged the shop recently to accommodate piano and violin recitals in the shop. I hope that he has progressed with his plan, as the setting seems just right for that kind of event. Let me know if you attend a recital.

Sandy's Books

Formerly known as Seasoned Booksellers, this shop is now *Sandy' Books*. It's a favorite of mine because I like to end a One-Day Bookstore-Tour here so I can enjoy the books and the food. Sandy's Books and Bakery is just that; equal parts read and eat. It's not just some muffins on a library cart. They

Sandy's Books - Rochester

have some real food and it's been real good each time. How can you resist buying a book about food when you are eating?

The owners have committed themselves to sustainable agriculture, and through various activities, they try to educate the public and bring their message to those who visit the shop or at events they hold away from the shop.

The Book Shed

When I stopped at *The Book Shed* during a recent visit, my wife went shopping across the street at the general store. It was the kind of store you could only find in the most rural parts of New

The Book Shed - Benson

77

England. When you are at The Book Shed, you are really rural. The shed is small and the aisles are narrow. But, the stacks are high and just the books on the floor waiting to be sorted and shelved makes the visit worthwhile. I never visit without finding several "must have's." My wife found some "must have's" across the street too.

The Country Bookshop

For nearly 40 years, this shop, just west of the Groton State Forest, has been sharing its 30,000 volume stock with rare book and ephemera collectors. Situated in an old house, the slightly cramped feeling is compounded by the various small rooms in which everything is stuffed. It's worth the effort of searching as you can be sure to find something of great interest at a fair price.

The Country Bookshop – St. Johnsbury

It seems that Plainfield is remote, but in reality it's not far from Montpelier or St. Johnsbury, unless you view those cities as remote from your location in downtown Boston, which is three hours away. It's all relative. If you are vacationing in Northern Vermont, this shop is worth making the trip.

78

Hermit Hill Books
95 Main Street
Poultney VT 05766
Tel: 802-287-5757
Web: hermithillbooks.com

Pleasant Street Books
48 Pleasant Street
Woodstock VT 05091
Tel: 802-457-4050
Web: pleasantstreetbooks.com

Sandy's Books
30 North Main Street
Rochester VT 05767
Tel: 802-767-4258
Web: seasonedbooks.com

The Book Shed
733 Lake Road
Benson VT 05731
Tel: 802-537-2190
Web: thebookshed.com

The Country Bookshop
35 Mill Street
Plainfield VT 05667
Tel: 802-454-8439
Web: thecountrybookshop.com

ONE-DAY BOOKSTORE-TOURS

A One-Day Bookstore-Tour is a fun way to map out a route that brings you into contact with three or four or more bookshops during a single round-robin tour. I read about the One-Day Bookstore Tour on Joseph Trenn's website. He wanted his website visitors to know about other worthy used and rare book shops in the region where he had his store.

This inspired me to take the tour and visit the shops that I hadn't been to before. They have now become regular stops for

Bearly Read Books – Sudbury MA

me when we visit Vermont on vacation. But, it also showed me that the same marketing technique that applies to McDonalds, Burger King and Wendys may apply to used books shops. If you cluster similar businesses together you create a "destination."

I think about the North End in Boston. As soon as I say it, I think about the restaurants, café's and bakeries that feature the same italian food. We all understand that the North End has a special meaning. It wouldn't be the same if there was only one café or restaurant.

I have made dozens of One-Day Bookstore-Tours on my own over the years, and in this section of the Guide I will share a few with you. My blog has more Tours.

Chapter Thirteen

One-Day Bookstore-Tour in Connecticut

Connecticut Coastline:
- *Harbor Books – Old Saybrook*
- *Book Barn – Niantic*
- *Book Trader, Etc. – Groton*
- *Bank Square Books – Mystic*

Finding Bargains Along
the Connecticut Coastline

My most recent One-Day Bookstore Tour took me to four of my favorite places along the Connecticut coastline. Starting with Harbor Books in Old Saybrook and ending at Bank Square Books in Mystic was only a drive of about 27 miles. Along the way I visited the Book Barn in Niantic and Book Trader Etc., in Groton. The Old Saybrook to Mystic (or Westerly RI) stretch is an historic and inviting tourist destination enjoyed by many, especially during the summer. The beaches, the parks, the country inns and historic sites, such as the Mystic seaport, are all strong attractions. Years ago, when I lived in Mystic, it seemed to me that the area was underrated as a destination and somewhat still is in my mind.

But, for me, the destination bookshops offer a great day trip for someone vacationing in the area. You can find a great collection of used books at three of the four stops, and while the Bank Square Books in Mystic is not a strong used book shop, it makes up for it with the emphasis on local authors and books about the sea, sailing and nautical interests. It also has a strong children's section.

Harbor Books

In Old Saybrook, *Harbor Books* is small but mighty. It has an eclectic mix of titles and I always manage to find something that I consider a bargain; either because it's ridiculously low priced, or it's an underpriced find. When I find something, such as an autographed book, it feels like a successful treasure hunt. It always intrigues me that the store owner has a constantly changing collection of books about Katherine Hepburn.

I picked up a first edition version of *ME*, by Katherine Hepburn, written in 1991.

Book Barn

Up the road in Niantic, the *Book Barn* is actually three separate locations, each with its own unique look and feel. But, you can rest assured that I bought books in all three locations. They are all within a minute's drive of each other; I suppose the really hearty could walk, but how could I carry all those books? The main barn had some great military genre books; the Midtown location had some great biographies; and the Downtown location had a recent arrival of movie star biographies that I couldn't resist. Plus, this was their annual 30 percent sale, so the low prices were even better.

If you are inclined to sell your books, this shop is more receptive than others, although they have a strict procedure, including passing out Position in Line cards for the early birds. If you get there early on a book-buying day, they issue a number

84

for your position in line so that you can continue browsing and determine where you will spend your earnings for the books you trade in.

On my most recent visit, they were warning visitors that one of the many cats was on a tirade and not to approach it. This is a bit unusual for bookstore cats. They generally have a mild disposition toward visitors, but something had set this one off and it's always wise to listen to the cat owner on such things.

The Book Trader, Etc.

Continuing eastward, I arrived in Groton, home of the submarine manufacturer, General Dynamics-Electric Boat. The *Book Trader, Etc.*, is a small store, sharing a plaza with Dunkin Donuts. In fact, they swapped locations when the doughnut shop wanted to add a drive-through. But, the book shop continues its decades-long tradition with its 3x5 card file for buyers who make a purchase and get a credit against their next purchase when they return the previous purchase. It's wild. I never get involved with that sort of thing because I shop in dozens of shops all over the place. But, for the locals, this is a great feature.

Bank Square Books

The final stop of the day was at *Bank Square Books* (see P.1) in Mystic. It's right downtown close to the drawbridge. You will find lots of local author and local interest books here. It's really great to see a full-service independent bookshop right in the middle of the action. It's one of my favorite bookstores. Now that the hard scape renovation of the streets is complete and we can navigate the sidewalks again, it's a great time to visit Mystic.

Chapter Fourteen

One-Day Bookstore-Tour in Maine

Maine Coastline Near Bar Harbor:
- *Sherman's Books - Bar Harbor*
- *Bar Harbor Bookshop - Hulls Cove*
- *Big Chicken Barn Bookshop - Ellsworth*

**Bar Harbor in the Fall is
A Rare Book Lover's Dream**

On our most recent fall vacation in Bar Harbor, Maine, we had the chance to play golf, drive to the top of Cadillac Mountain (twice) and enjoy the beauty and majesty of Acadia Park, including Thunder Hole. We hadn't been there recently, and while many things were the same, others were different. The last time we visited we stayed at one of the historic inns downtown. This time we opted for a more luxurious resort hotel with all the extra features. Either way can be an ideal choice for visiting Bar Harbor.

One of the days was a bit overcast and some showers were predicted so we made it our "shopping" day. We always expect one day on vacation to be a chance to run through the various quaint shops or nearby outlet malls to find some bargains. I managed to weave one of my One-Day Bookstore-Tours into the shopping day. Some of the bookstores were places I have visited on previous visits, and delightfully, there were some new stops as well. It's my experience that a vacation in New England is always enhanced by seeking out the unusual rural book shop.

This book store tour took me to *Sherman's Books*, the *Mystery Cove Book Shop*, and the *Big Chicken Barn Books*. I had planned to stop in at *Mr. Paperback*, but even though we drove by it, our "shopping" day diverted me from a visit there. Unfortunately, they have since closed after operating in Ellsworth for over 30 years.

Sherman's Books

Sherman's Books is at 56 Main Street, right in the heart of downtown Bar Harbor. During our week there I must have walked past it a dozen times and stepped inside four or five times. I know I bought books at least twice there that week. On my official One-Day Bookstore-Tour day I concentrated on the discount book island. It's amazing what you can find. It ranged from cook books to children's books to local author photo books.

The Sherman's Books and Stationary chain has three other locations: Boothbay Harbor, Camden and Freeport, Maine. I've been to all of them and each has its own quirky look and charm that you hope to find in locally owned shops in vacation destination cities and towns. At the Bar Harbor store, the collection of discounted children's books was amazing. Finding something for the kids to read while they are on vacation is always important. It's great in the evenings or for the car ride home. It's also an economical keepsake of the vacation for the kids. Instead of a candy bar shaped like a Moose, a book is a much better purchase.

Bar Harbor Book Shop

My second stop of the bookstore tour was at the Mystery Cove Book Shop about three miles up the road in Hulls Cove. Today, the shop goes by the name, *Bar Harbor Book Shop*. For me the "mystery" was how anyone could find this place. At the time of my visit there was no Internet address listing. Today, their website shows the address as 1 Dewey St, "500 feet up Crooked Road." The GPS was able to get me to Dewey Street, so the "mystery" was solved. But, after all that effort, it sure was a relief to find a charming used book store that I could have shopped in for an hour. I made off with a carton filled with books, but I left a lot on the table this day. I will definitely be back to this shop.

Big Chicken Barn Book Shop

Just a bit out of town in Ellsworth, Maine, the *Big Chicken Barn Book Shop* loomed large on the side of the road. And I do mean large. It is really unbelievable. Today, with modern plumbing installed, the barn offers convenient, comfortable indoor facilities. That makes the extended time you will spend here a lot more enjoyable. You need time when visiting here because the place is enormous. The upstairs is lined with aisles of books to meet all your reading requirements. The biographies and Americana sections were filled with books. I relieved the owners of a few of them so they could put more books up on the shelves for others. I'm courteous that way. The pricing was fair, so it was easy to load up on biographies, history, political commentary, and at least one novel for my wife.

Chapter Fifteen

One-Day Bookstore-Tour in Massachusetts

Middlesex County Massachusetts:
- *Bearly Read Books - Sudbury*
- *Willow Books - Acton*
- *Second Hand Prose - Acton*
- *The Concord Book Shop - Concord*
- *Barrow Book Shop - Concord*

**The Book Shop Heard 'round the World or
How I Spent a Day near Concord-Lexington**

The historic sites in Massachusetts are boundless. When we take a day trip to visit an historic site, such as the North Bridge in Concord, I try to scope out a reason to return on another day for a visit to several book shops. Recently, I made a circle trip to several bookstores, including some I had not been to before.

The trip started off with a thunk as I discovered that *Annie's Book Stop* and Espresso Paulo in Framingham were completely abandoned. The whole plaza was mostly deserted so maybe they moved somewhere else. But, further down the road toward Framingham the *Book Cellar* was closed too. So, it was early in the day and I was zero for two. Not a good start.

To console myself, I stopped at Trader Joe's and bought a case of wine. (For three dollars a bottle, it's hard to beat.)

Bearly Read Books

I left the buzziness of Route 9 via peaceful, tree-lined Edgell Road towards Route 20, where I got to *Bearly Read Books* in Sudbury about 10 minutes before they opened. After an hour I had *seen* three book shops and been inside none. Thankfully, they opened at their scheduled time of 10 AM.

The shop has been around for about 25 years, with the new owners operating it for the past five years. It's an impressive antiquarian and rare book shop with about 40,000 books on hand, but it also has more generic used books, and some at very reasonable prices. They also have a great section of signed books.

I got *The Hellfire Club* by Peter Straub and *Inadmissible Evidence* by Philip Friedman. Even though the owners were away, the person minding the store was helpful and knowledgeable.

Willow Books

I left Bearly Read Books and proceeded toward Acton, about 20 minutes away, to *Willow Books*. I hadn't been there before, but had meant to stop in. It's a large building, which they share with an insurance company. The store was bright and cheerful. It reminded me of Tatnuck Booksellers in Westborough. It has a café for coffee and a muffin, clean rest rooms, and a big kids section. There was a good display of local authors and near the front door was a big section filled with bargain books.

The used book section is strictly paperbacks, so it was not interesting to me. But, if that's what you are looking for, you can get started on buying and selling books back to them for credits on future purchases. That's great for the locals, not so much for vacationers to the region.

I picked up *The Last Founding Father: James Monroe* by Harlow Giles Unger. I had previously read his book about Lafayette. I also got *The Battle for God* by Karen Armstrong. Both books were $6.98 in the bargain rack. I picked up some other books as well. The day was getting better.

Second Hand Prose

Just a few minutes up the road I got to *Second Hand Prose*. The shop has been there for over 20 years. It's got a nice selection of paperback and hard cover books. It offers an interesting buy-back program where you get one sixth of the cover price for books you turn in and eventually get your purchase price down to one fourth the cover price based on credits you've earned. Don't worry; they will explain how it works. The hundreds of customers that have cards on file are testimony to the successful discount strategy.

I picked up *Benjamin Franklin* by Edmond Morgan and Rabbi Kushner's book *For Those Who Can't Believe.*

The Concord Book Shop

The last stop of the day was in Concord. To get there I had to go through the infamous Concord Traffic Rotary. *The Concord Book Shop* is one of my favorite bookstores. I include it in my book, *A Vacationer's Guide to Rural New England Bookstores.* The shop has all the latest books, a deep selection of history, politics, nature, and especially biographies, which is a strong interest of mine. I picked up Stephen Greenblatt's, *The*

Swerve, How The World Became Modern; a Pulitzer Prize winner. I also stepped outside and visited another of my favorite book shops: *Barrow Book Store*.

Barrow Book Store

This used and rare book shop, which is practically next door to The Concord Book Shop, specializes in Concord authors such as Thoreau, Hawthorne, and Emerson. I bought half a dozen books on this visit. Three were signed by the authors. There were a few that I left behind for the next visit.

One of the books was in a glass case and the shop keeper opened it for me to inspect. The signature was not an inscription, rather, it was a card associated with a book signing. The price was fair, but it wasn't the type of book I collected.

Chapter Sixteen

One-Day Bookstore-Tour in Massachusetts

Massachusetts' Quaint North Shore:
- *Manchester by the Book – Manchester by the Sea*
- *Toad Hall Bookstore – Rockport*
- *The Bookstore of Gloucester – Gloucester*
- *Jabberwocky – Newburyport*

My One-Day Bookstore-Tour Through
Massachusetts' Quaint North Shore

About three years ago, sometime after John Updike died, I made one of my regular passes through the North Shore and visited several of my favorite bookstores. When I stopped at *Manchester-by-the-Book*, in Manchester-by-the-Sea, the owner had stacked every possible book written by John Updike into a tower of books standing in the middle of the store. He had placed a For Sale sign of $1000 for the entire 48 book collection. I have to admit I had not seen this merchandizing tactic previously – or since – but, it still looms fresh in my mind. Just for point of clarification, I did not make the purchase.

But, while I was there I examined the precariously stacked tribute to Updike and counted off how many of his books I had in my personal library. Not enough. Visually, the number of books in that pile was amazing. So, since that day as I went about to various book stores, I have sought out the best bargains

on the books needed for my own tower of tribute to Updike. I'm
still working on that.

Manchester by the Book

On a more recent visit to *Manchester-by-the-Book*, I found
an Abbie Hoffman book, written by his brother Jack Hoffman,
Run, Run, Run, which included references to an Interview that
Teresa Hannifin had with Abbie as a newspaper reporter. I had
read the book a long time ago, but had misplaced it, so I bought
this to restore my collection of books by people I actually know,
or books with people mentioned in it that I actually know. (Not
as impressive as the Updike tower, but it's something.)

Toad Hall Bookstore

Anyway, upon leaving Manchester-by-the-Sea, I moved on
to Rockport, which was about 20 minutes for the 10 mile trip.
Here I stopped in at the *Toad Hall Bookstore*. I love the circular
staircase up to the bargain area. There were books here for $3
that I had recently seen in other stores at non-discounted prices. I
found Tim Russerts' *Wisdom of our Fathers* in pristine condition
for $3. Even if you buy it on Amazon for one cent, the delivery
charge is $3.95; and you won't know its condition until it
arrives. Forget that.

Amazon's No Bargain

Another book found was *The Culture of War* by Martin L.
Van Creveld for $3. Amazon has it for $4.95 plus shipping. And
another: *Waking Giant: America in the Age of Jackson* by David
S. Reynolds. Amazon has it for $4.30 plus shipping. By the way,
the Amazon books are paperback and the books at Toad Hall

were hardcover and pristine. I hope I am making my point. Just because it's at Amazon does not make it a bargain.

The Bookstore of Gloucester

I moved on from Rockport to Gloucester on a slight backtrack direction. It was only about five miles and 12 minutes to get to the center of town. Parking is generally easier than you think if you are willing to glide around for a while to snag a meter. The *Book Store of Gloucester* is one street up from the waterfront. You can't go wrong at the 40 percent off table. *My Ears are Bent* by Joseph Mitchell caught my eye. Out of print since this collection of his writing was published in 1938; this was a real find – and a real bargain.

The Clam's the Thing

The final leg of this trip took me up through Essex, Ipswich and Rowley toward Newburyport. Along the way I stopped at one of the clam boxes in Ipswich. (It's pretty much a local ordinance that you have to stop and eat at a clam box). I also went by Cape Ann Golf Course, a place I frequent when my wife is on a two-tank scuba dive off Front Beach in Rockport. Now you know why I get to make this Bookstore-Tour so often.

Jabberwocky

Anyway, my final bookstore for the day was *Jabberwocky* in Newburyport. This is the place where I strain my neck reading the books on the extra-tall shelves. But, the bargain bins and the Green Room make up for that slight discomfort. The store is well stocked and the sections are labeled well enough that you can find what you need without having to ask, which is good because the place is always busy and the staff may be tied up. On a recent visit I found *One Man's America* by George Will, *MacArthur's Victory* by Harry Gailey, and at a great discount, a collection of John Cheever stories.

Chapter Seventeen

One-Day Bookstore-Tour in New Hampshire

New Hampshire's Portsmouth Region:
- *River Run Bookstore – Portsmouth*
- *Drake Farm Books – North Hampton*
- *The Book Outlet – North Hampton*

One-Day Bookstore-Tour Yields
Great Book Bargains in Portsmouth Area

I just got back from a great One-Day Bookstore-Tour in and around Portsmouth NH, where the *RiverRun Bookstore* reopened at its new location. On Saturday, the place was buzzing. I was disappointed to learn that the SecondRun shop, which has been closed for a year won't be reopening any time soon. But, according to the one of the owners, there may be a Used Book store in its future – but, probably out of town where the rents are lower.

River Run Bookstore
The new shop is delightful. It's not very large, but well organized and thankfully, it's peppered with a lot of used books. Unlike a lot of shops, the new and used books are inter-mixed on the same shelves by category. So, when I'm looking at biographies, I can find a new release parked right next to a used copy of *Amelia Earhart* by Doris Rich for $10. Now, that's what I'm talking about. I also found *The River of Doubt*, a great

99

biography about Theodore Roosevelt's adventure on the Amazon River for the same price. They also have bargain books in boxes at the front of the store from $2 to $5.

Downtown Portsmouth is a great walking town, but you don't have to walk far to find shops, restaurants, bar and grille, galleries, and a lot more. I visited the former location of the SecondRun used book shop, which now anchored an artist's gallery. Then, after a quick bite at The Page Restaurant, I was on my way seven miles up the road to Drake Farm in North Hampton.

The Drake Farm Book Shop

The Drake Farm Book Shop is a remarkable local landmark. The barn was built around 1830 and from its antique railroad station wood stove (this weekend's only source of heat) to its two floors overstuffed with 45,000 books, you know you are visiting someplace special. The owner, Bob, greets everyone who enters and encouraged browsers to button up their overcoat as the barn is unheated due to the $300 per week oil charge. So, bring your gloves and when you can't stand it anymore, come back to the store front and warm yourself at the wood stove.

The $300 oil charge is understandable once you get inside the enormous barn. Room after room draws you further along into the enormous space. Books are stacked on shelves so tightly that you have to pull out several books at a time to release the one you want to inspect. The rooms and sections of rooms are well labeled so you can find the military or natural science or fiction sections easily. But, this is clearly a place that requires more than one visit. The vastness of the collections is hard to describe.

Among the several books that I bought was *Marshall, Hero for Our Times* by Leonard Mosley. The collection of WW II and other military genre books was impressive. For the most part, each book is wrapped in plastic with a written description of edition and pricing. The books are handled less this way and better preserved for the ultimate buyer. Each of the several books I purchased was a First Edition and each was treated by the bookseller with care and reverence. The pricing was fair and if you group your buys, you can earn some further discounts for purchases over $50 and $100, etc. So a good deal becomes a great deal.

The Book Outlet

Moving on down the road, you will find the *Book Outlet* just a mile away. This is another landmark, in its own way, as it's been a fixture at the North Hampton Village Shopping Center at the Intersection of Rte. 1 and Rte. 111, for over a decade. The shop features paperback and hardcover used books and accepts book trade-ins toward purchases. It's clean, neat and well lit. When you spot the $1.99 and $2.99 orange tags on books in the History or Biography section, or the $0.99 box at the front of the store, it's hard to believe your luck. I'm always tempted to fill my arms with books. I found four volumes today that set me back a total of about $10. Among them were a book by Henry Kissinger, *The Fitzgerald's and Kennedy's* saga by Doris Kearns Goodwin, and the biography of *Whittaker Chambers* by Sam Tanenhaus.

Normally I can stop at four or five book shops in a day, but the extra browsing in downtown Portsmouth and the extended visit to Drake Farm limited me to three shops. Not that I'm complaining, the visits were all worthwhile. I also devoted a little bit of time to a Valentine gift for my wife. It's important for future touring expeditions to maintain a happy home.

Chapter Eighteen

One-Day Bookstore-Tour in Vermont

Woodstock Vermont:
The Yankee Bookshop - Woodstock
Shiretown Books - Woodstock
Pleasant Street Books - Woodstock

It's only a couple hours north from my home to reach the town of Woodstock VT, which is a preferred destination for many reasons. The town is beautiful in any season, the main street is lined with charming shops and galleries, the dining and drinking options are numerous, and I can find a library and three book shops within walking distance of each other. Now, that's a great reason to visit any town.

The *Norman Williams Public Library* had a book sale this past weekend ranging from 50 cents to a few dollars each on a great collection of hard cover and soft cover books. My wife selected a novel and I found two non-fiction hard covers that totaled $8. The library was happy and we were delighted.

The Yankee Bookshop
A few short steps down the street was the *The Yankee Bookshop*, notable for its bright yellow awning. They claim to be the oldest continuously operated independent bookshop in town, having first opened in 1935. The shop is small but well organized. The book selection was wide ranging and I was able to find some titles that I had to have. I also appreciated the rack

of local newspapers at the front of the store. It's amazing to me that more book shops don't bother with offering the local periodicals.

Shiretown Books

A few more steps up the street brought us to *Shiretown Books*. The shop has begun to mingle new and used books on the same shelf. This is a great idea. I prefer to make my selections in the history, biography and political commentary section from used titles because a book about an historical event two hundred years ago, that was written by someone 10 years ago, is still fresh to me. Obviously, if you want to read an analysis of last year's election, it's necessary to buy at new book prices. I found two volumes at $4.95 each. So, for fewer than ten dollars I had a biography of *Thurgood Marshall* and *Mary Queen of Scots* by Antonia Fraser. Another good day as a result of used book pricing.

Pleasant Street Books

The final stop for the day was at *Pleasant Street Books*. It was a short ride/walk up the road and was the main reason we came on today's visit. The antiquarian and rare book shop operated by Sonny Saul has thousands of books, many of which are first editions. The shop resides in a restored barn behind his house, along the river. It's quintessential in its charm, inside and out. The inside has undergone a significant change over the past year. Sonny cleared out a lot of books on the ground level to make room for a piano and seating that can accommodate recitals. Although no formal schedule exists, I think we will be hearing (excuse the weak pun) more about it soon.

The rare books mingle with the merely used books. I like both types. For those looking for Shakespeare folios, he has some. For those looking for *Foucault's Pendulum* by Umberto Eco, the cost was only $8. For the Shakespeare, a bit more. I bought the Umberto Eco volume.

The upstairs section is more crowded than downstairs. The books are stacked from floor to ceiling, but Sonny has provided numerous low stools for visitors to hunch down comfortably to scan the treasures on the bottom shelves. I think I bought seven books, but I could easily have bought many more. Each aisle had something to peak my reading interest. Other aisles had volumes that peaked my collecting instinct. Sometimes my instincts get the best of me. This day I settled for the seven, which included one signed copy, a few first editions and a few readers. Excellent.

Generally, a One-Day Bookstore-Tour takes in a few nearby towns, but this time I never left the boundaries of Woodstock VT. In between the visits we took lunch at the *Woodstock Inn* and some libations at *Bentley's* downtown. Both were fun, but the drinks are cheaper at Bentley's, believe me.

Chapter Nineteen

One-Day Bookstore-Tour in Vermont

Along Vermont's Route 7:
- *Otter Creek Used Books*
- *Monroe Street Books*
- *Flying Pig Bookstore*
- *Crow Bookshop*

Rutland VT to Burlington VT is about 68 miles. The trip along Route 7 would take almost two hours as the road is not exactly a super highway. But, in the pursuit of book shops along the way, I managed to turn it into a five hour journey. Once we got to Burlington, some rain showers emerged and we dodged into and out of the shops downtown – where of all things I found another book shop. (My wife suspects I knew it was there all along; but, it really was a surprise.) Our return trip to Rutland, where we were staying during this visit to Vermont made it a long day. But, I would say it was a satisfying day.

On the way out of Rutland we had breakfast at the Midway Diner, where the eggs benedict featured a great Canadian bacon. The traditional looking diner is something we look for when we travel and this one didn't disappoint. We scooted out onto Route 7 after we ate and took off north.

It took about 25 minutes to travel 17 miles north to Brandon, where we stopped at the *Briggs Carriage Bookstore*. Sadly, it was closed. And according to the recorded message on the telephone it is permanently closed. I don't know exactly when this happened, but it was certainly sad to discover this bad news at our first stop. So we plunged on to hopefully better results up Route 7.

Otter Creek Used Books

Our next stop was Middlebury, about another 20 minutes on Route 7. *The Otter Creek Used Books* shop is now at 99 Maple St. It gave up its Main Street location and I really like the new one. It's a bit hard to find at first, as you have to turn down a tight driveway, but it's worth it once you get there. The owner claims it's still not really organized the way she would like it, but trust me when I say, it is way ahead of a lot of other places when it comes to sorting and labeling.

I especially liked some of the walk-in closets that featured various categories, such as gardening and antiquarian. I found a signed copy of *Bookbanning in America* by William Noble. It was a bargain, which I confirmed on the Internet when I got home from vacation. I also found *The Path to Power* by Margaret Thatcher for $5. This book is her account of her personal life and how she became involved in politics. Reviewers claim it's better than her book, *The Downing Street Years*. I'll keep my eyes open for that one too.

Monroe Street Books

Further up Route 7 about two miles was *Monroe Street Books*. The warehouse appearance, both outside and inside, seems appropriate as the shop is co-located with a storage locker company. It appears that the biggest customer is the book shop. Over 80,000 books are stacked on shelves so high you need a ladder to get up and read the top rows. I found Robert Dallek's

Nixon and Kissinger for a reasonable price and it turned out today all political books were on sale with an extra 25 percent discount. Dallek's known for his writing about Kennedy, Johnson, Reagan and Roosevelt. I can't wait to read this one. It was time for lunch. I had to promise my wife that the next stop would include lunch. So, we headed to Vergennes and the *3 Squares Café,* still on Route 7. This place was classic small town Main Street café. The tables don't match. The chairs don't match. The open kitchen behind the deli-style glass front counter gives the impression of a cafeteria, delicatessen, coffee shop and bistro, all in one. Don't forget the local brewed beer. And I didn't. It was great. So were the sandwiches. When my wife ordered the Mimosa, we saw the waitress run down the street to buy some Champagne. The drink came in a tall water glass instead of the traditional six ounce flute. The freshness of the ingredients and the presentation was gourmet, without the gourmet price. It's a definite repeat stop for us.

Alas, there did not appear to be a book shop, but along Main Street one of the shops, which appeared to be a consignment place, had a sign declaring books by the pound. They were selling books by their weight. The price was two pounds of used books for a dollar? This I had to see. And sure enough, stacked up on the floor, tables, shelves and everywhere they could find a spot were books. And in the front window was a scale for you to determine how many pounds of books you were hauling.

Sweet Charity

It turns out we were in the *Sweet Charity* resale shop. Proceeds from the shop support families in need locally. Their

109

website is sweetcharityVT.com. Their motto is "if you are downsizing keep us in mind." I don't know if the books are a one-time event, or if they sell books on a regular basis. But, if it goes on regularly, it's a great place for bargains, while doing something helpful at the same time. I took quite a heavy load out myself, including *Lake Wobegon Days* by Garrison Keillor and *David Brinkley, a Memoir*.

Flying Pig Bookstore

Full of pastrami, beer, and books, we took off from Vergennes toward Shelburne, about 20 minutes further up Route 7. In Shelburne, we stopped at the *Flying Pig Bookstore*, which is in the same building as the Bearded Frog Bar and Grill. You have to give them credit for two eclectic retail names. Flying Pig and Bearded Frog?

The Flying Pig carries about 40,000 volumes and has a tremendous focus on children's books. There seemed to be a lot of variety and the store was well organized. The shop publishes its own newsletter, *Pig-Tales*, which features books for kids, by age group; books written by Vermont authors, and other categories. To publish a 16 page quarterly newsletter is very impressive. It's definitely worth reading. Shelburne is a destination all to itself. You could spend more than a day here taking in the sights. We will be back as soon as possible.

The final leg of today's trip was 15 minutes north to Burlington. We've been here before and it's always a delight to visit. The open air Church Street Marketplace is what we wish all downtowns looked like. The traffic is limited to a few cross-over points, but essentially it has become a walker's paradise. The shops and cafés overflow onto the brick sidewalks and

110

plazas giving a chance to everyone to enjoy the fresh air, the sun and the general hustle-bustle of a vibrant marketplace.

Crow Bookshop

We took advantage of the Ben & Jerry's ice cream shop, as my wife has made Coffee Coffee Buzz Buzz her favorite. As we continued our rounds we found the *Crow Bookshop* at 14 Church St. In previous trips I hadn't really bumped into the place, but I liked it very much. They are mostly a used book shop, but they have new titles as well. The used books are 50 percent off or better and the new books are also discounted. I got *Darwin's Armada* by Iain McCalman for $12. The cover price is $29.95. That's definitely more than 50 percent off. I also got *The Canal Builders* by Julie Greene at the same discount.

So, at the end of the day our One-Day Bookstore-Tour took us to four great book shops. Although one of the planned stops was closed, we found an unexpected one to fill out our dance card.

Website Resources
for
Antiquarian Book Associations

MAINE
Maine Antiquarian Booksellers Association
mainebooksellers.org

MASSACHUSETTS – RHODE ISLAND
Massachusetts and Rhode Island Antiquarian Booksellers
mariab.org

NEW HAMPSHIRE
New Hampshire Antiquarian Booksellers Association
nhaba.org

VERMONT
Vermont Antiquarian Booksellers Association
vermontisbookcountry.com

About the Author

Richard F. Wright lives in Jefferson, Massachusetts with his wife, Patti, and from this central location views all of New England as his backyard. Within a few hours he can reach any of hundreds of book shops where he can find the exact book he didn't know he was looking for.

His range of interests include all books about books, biographies of celebrities and important historical characters, whether famous or infamous, mostly hard-cover, signed by the author if possible, and certainly at the best price. There is nothing more attractive than a remainder shelf or a bargain bin.

His website: *GuideToNewEnglandBookstores.com* and his Blog: *Richard-Wright.Blogspot.com* both focus on keeping awareness high concerning the prospects for the rural book shop in New England. He welcomes the continued support of readers and book collectors that will balance their investment between online sources and the brick and mortar sources.

His *A Vacationer's Guide to Rural New England Bookstores* was first published in 2008 and the current edition was released in 2012. The website attempts to update changes among the openings, moving, and closings of book shops in New England.

CPSIA information can be obtained at www.ICGtesting.com
Printed in the USA
LVOW071106080213

319234LV00002B/247/P